THE TIMES

QUIZ BOOK

THE TIMES
QUIZ BOOK

Howard Robin and Tom Kremer

TIMES BOOKS

ACKNOWLEDGEMENTS

Page 208 A Camera Press Ltd, London
          B Central Press Photos Ltd, London
Page 209 C Joanna Ney, The Film Society of Lincoln Center, New York
Page 210 E and Page 214 Radio Times Hulton Picture Library, London
Page 210 F G. F. Street, Lincs
Page 211 G Associated Press, London
          H UPI, London
Page 212 I Keystone
          J P. A. Reuters, London
          K The Times
Page 213 L The Times
          M The Times
Page 214 O The Times
Page 215 P Paul Popper Ltd, London
          R Kobal Collection, London
Page 216 S Press Association, London
          T Royal Astronomical Society, London

CIP Data
Robin Howard
  The Times Quiz Book
  1. Questions and answers
  I. Title. II. Kremer, Tom
  793.73   AG195

Published by Times Books Limited, 16 Golden Square, London, W1R 4BN

Copyright © Howard Robin and Tom Kremer, 1987

ISBN 0 7230 0302 5

Typeset by London Post (Printers) Ltd

Printed and bound in Great Britain by The Guernsey Press Co. Ltd, Guernsey, Channel Islands

CONTENTS

Authors' note

In writing this quiz we have tried to go beyond merely testing factual knowledge and set questions also to evoke interest and entertain.

There are questions difficult enough to test the expert and their extensive range should provide an enjoyable challenge to a wider public.

For variety and ease of use the book has 11 sections, according to subject matter. Each section is divided into individual quizzes of 15 questions (except for the picture section which has 50 questions). This arrangement lends the book naturally to games for groups and competitive scoring.

We have endeavoured to be as accurate as possible making use of standard works of reference. However, the quiz format itself and the limitation of space must lead to the occasional oversimplification. We leave the resolution of any ambiguities that may have arisen to the good sense of the reader.

We would like to express our gratitude to J.A. Stein for his constructive criticism and advice.

Howard Robin   Tom Kremer

1 What are googols and googolplexes?

2 Who wrote *Totem and Taboo* and who wrote *Le Totémisme aujourd'hui*?

3 What is Pinyin?

4 Which system of construction was used on the Sydney Harbour bridge: suspension, cantilever or steel arch?

5 Who is traditionally regarded as the founder of Taoism?

6 What was the mythological home of the Scandinavian gods reached by the bridge of the rainbow?

7 What is a quasar?

8 How does the Fabian Society get its name?

9 To whom was the term *Eminence Grise* first applied?

10 What do the colours of the French tricolour represent?

11 What is an oxymoron?

12 Which arts movement was launched in 1909 by Filippo Marinetti?

13 Where and when was the Encyclopaedia Britannica first published?

14 What is the name of the country previously called Nyasaland?

15 Which subjects comprised the 'Trivium'?

1 Name four of the nine Greek Muses.

2 What does an otorhinolaryngologist treat?

3 Who painted 'The Garden of Earthly Delights'?

4 Where would you find an alexandrine?

5 What do the names 'Butts' and 'Fletcher' have in common?

6 Which horse won the 1987 Grand National?

7 What object is inscribed 'Cormac McCarthy *fortis me fieri facit* AD 1446'; and what does it mean?

8 To which language family do Finnish and Hungarian belong?

9 Who was the first Yorkist King of England?

10 What is the colouring of an Airedale terrier?

11 Who founded the Berliner Ensemble?

12 Who founded RADA?

13 What does 'Mahatma' mean?

14 What is a "roman à clef"?

15 What do the intials 'sfz' indicate in music?

MIXED BAG QUESTIONS

1 In increasing order of abundance, what are the four most abundant gases in the earth's atmosphere.

2 How many cards are there in the Greater Arcana of the modern Tarot pack?

3 In Norse mythology, what is the name of the ash tree that supports the universe and what is the name of the giant from whose body the world is created?

4 Which influential group of French artists took their name from a Hebrew word meaning 'prophets'?

5 What is the currency of Ecuador?

6 What is the currency of Korea?

7 After whom is Somerville College, Oxford, named?

8 What are the three basic parts of a typical comet?

9 In 19th-century Britain, who was 'The Railway King'?

10 What was a *kithara*?

11 What was the approximate population of the world in 1650?

12 How does Tuesday get its name?

13 What does the name 'Alhambra' signify in Arabic?

14 Who devised and founded judo?

15 In pottery what is a 'pelike'?

1 What is psittacosis?

2 Which is closer to modern man: Peking man or Cro-Magnon man?

3 Which language does the word 'pyjama' come from?

4 Name the Seven Wonders of the Ancient World.

5 Who was the alleged son of Solomon and the Queen of Sheba, from whom the Falashas claim descent?

6 A hennin was a popular item of attire in the Renaissance period. What was it?

7 What is the capital of Madagascar?

8 What name do geologists generally give to the epoch that started 10,000 years ago and which includes the present?

9 Who was Mick the Miller?

10 What is the connection between the painting 'The Last of England' (1855) and the novel *The Good Soldier* (1915)?

11 What was the Decembrist Conspiracy and when did it take place?

12 Who said of whom 'Oh! he is mad is he? Then I wish he would bite some other of my generals'?

13 What was the capital of Tamerlane's empire?

14 Who composed the score to Olivier's film *Richard III*?

15 Which does not belong and why? Tu Fu, Kuo Hsi, Li Po.

MIXED BAG QUESTIONS

1 Place in ascending order: Viscounts, Marquesses, Barons, Dukes, Earls.

2 What does Labanotation record?

3 What is the religion of the Parsees of India?

4 Who first climbed the Matterhorn?

5 Where would you find the Boehm system?

6 Which living language do linguists consider to be most closely related to English?

7 What name was given to the cold room in a Roman baths?

8 Who were the two athletes portrayed in the film *Chariots of Fire*?

9 Who founded the city of Agade and has been called 'the first great imperialist in history'?

10 Who sculpted the (now lost) statue of Zeus at Olympia?

11 Of what did Gustav Mahler remark 'Fortissimo at last!'?

12 Who founded the Moscow Art Theatre and when?

13 What is the specific political meaning of 'disestablishment'?

14 Who was 'Chief of the Beautiful River'?

15 What is the official language of Ethiopia?

1 Who founded the Ballets Russes?

2 Who were the pacemakers in the first sub four-minute mile? ✓

3 Which geological period came between the Triassic and the Cretaceous?

4 Who wrote *The City of God*?

5 What was the landing area for the first manned moon landing?

6 What does stapedectomy involve?

7 What kind of animal is a Lippizaner?

8 What was the name of the first ship to sail around the world?

9 Who built the Panama Canal?

10 Describe the Liberian flag.

11 Who was Phillip Melancthon?

12 Name the first three months in the French Republican calendar?

13 What are Fraunhofer lines?

14 What is the origin of the word 'draconian'?

15 With whom did Bertrand Russell write the *Principia Mathematica*?

1 What are the Croonian, the Bakerian and the Wilkins?

2 What did a Pharaoh's double crown represent?

3 In which film did Marlene Dietrich sing *See What The Boys in the Back Room Will Have*?

4 Which doesn't belong: Osiris, Ptah, Kut, Horus, Set?

5 Who said: 'Everything failed me just at the moment when everything had succeeded'?

6 Which was the first aeroplane to fly faster than the speed of sound?

7 Who wrote the poems *The Giaour* and *The Prisoner of Chillon*?

8 Of which country was 'Foxy' Ferdinand the Tsar?

9 On which story is the film *2001: A Space Odyssey* based?

10 Which three goddesses were 'judged' by Paris?

11 Explain the relationships between Agamemnon, Menelaus, Helen and Clytemnestra.

12 Who are the Tuareg?

13 What are the two brightest stars in the sky?

14 Who directed the classic (1922) version of the vampire film *Nosferatu*?

15 What is nephology?

1 What name did the ancient Greeks give to amber?

2 What is the name of the Royal House of Sweden?

3 Who wrote *The Decline of the West*?

4 What name is given to the tiny air sacs in the lungs which re-oxygenate the blood?

5 What exactly is majolica?

6 What was a *bucintoro*?

7 Which conductor starred in *Fantasia*?

8 Who killed the playwright Joe Orton?

9 What is a bobolink?

10 Where and when did the first successful detonation of a hydrogen bomb occur?

11 Who wrote both *The Kreutzer Sonata* and *Resurrection*?

12 Who was 'Q'?

13 Who founded Positivism and coined the term 'sociology'?

14 Where was Charlemagne buried?

15 What name is given to The Conference on Science and World Affairs?

1 What are the three basic weapons used in fencing?

2 How is 21 expressed as a binary number?

3 Who was the first Prime Minister of the Union of South Africa?

4 Who wrote the novel *Zorba the Greek*?

5 Where was the Royal Greenwich Observatory moved to after World War II?

6 Where is Rupert Brooke buried?

7 What are the three novels of Samuel Beckett's trilogy?

8 Who wrote *The Abraham Lincoln Symphony*?

9 Where is the Teatro la Fenice?

10 Which sport was written about in *The Changing Room*?

11 Who were the two presidents of the Weimar Republic?

12 Which States border Wyoming?

13 What was the name of Alexander the Great's famous horse?

14 Whom did Alexander Pope satirize in the character Atticus?

15 Who is the Director General of the BBC and who were his last two predecessors?

1 What is the commonly given explanation for the early use of a fish as a symbol for Christ in Christian art and literature?

2 Who illustrated the celebrated work *The Birds of America*?

3 Where is the deltoid muscle? ✓

4 Who painted 'Van Gogh Painting Sunflowers'?

5 As members of which company did Nureyev, Makarova and Baryshnikov defect?

6 Who wrote *A Counterblaste to Tobacco*?

7 Who designed the Crystal Palace?

8 For what is the Ypsilanti family renowned?

9 What is the Munsell system?

10 Who was the president of South Vietnam from 1955 until 1963?

11 Who is generally credited with the invention of cribbage?

12 Who wrote the novel *Quo Vadis*?

13 What is the capital of Costa Rica?

14 What are the Greek equivalents for Juno, Mercury, Diana and Minerva?

15 How old are the cave paintings of Lascaux?

1 Who was governor of Roman Britain in AD 80?

2 Whose teachings did the Lollards follow?

3 What is the longest river of the Iberian peninsula?

4 Which international institution originated at a London coffee house in 1688?

5 Who wrote the screenplay for the film *Doctor Zhivago*?

6 What were the former names of Harare, Maputo and Kinshasa?

7 Which school produced Byron, Sheridan, Trollope and Galsworthy?

8 What is the opposite of a utopia?

9 Who were the Villanovans?

10 What are the currencies of Hungary and Yugoslavia?

11 Who said 'genius is one-per-cent inspiration and ninety-nine-per-cent perspiration'?

12 Who discovered Fiji in 1643?

13 Where and in which year was the decisive French defeat in Indo-China?

14 What was the real name of the writer Saki?

15 On which course is the US Masters golf tournament held?

1 Who were the father and grandfather of Zeus?

2 Which seas are linked by the Dardanelles? ✓

3 What is the name of the Norwegian parliament?

4 What is the difference between an isobar and an isotherm?

5 At which city was the tomb of King Mausolus built?

6 Who was the first Stuart king of Scotland?

Stewart

7 What is *kyudo*?

8 Who said 'A great empire and little minds go ill together'?

9 What is CERN?

10 For what is Thucydides most famous?

11 What is the lowest hand in standard poker?

12 What is an 'iatrogenic' disease?

13 At which college did Newton, Wittgenstein and Byron all study?

14 Where is Graham Sutherland's 'Christ in His Majesty'?

15 What is H_2O_2?

1 What was John Napier's famous invention?

2 Who built the first tunnel under the River Thames?

3 Who founded the Peripatetic school of philosophy?

4 What are the three capitals of South Africa?

5 What is 'gesso'?

6 Name the three gods that comprise the Hindu triad, the Trimurti.

7 What crosses the synaptic cleft?

8 What is the origin of the word tulip?

9 Which word denotes a chief magistrate of ancient Athens?

10 Who founded the Jesuit Order?

11 Which race is recognised as the supreme championship of English steeplechasing?

12 Which European state first settled the Falkland Islands?

13 What was Dante's full name?

14 What is the largest active volcano?

15 Of which country is St. Wenceslas the patron saint?

1 Very high numbers. A googol is the number one followed by a hundred zeros. A googolplex is the number one followed by a googol zeros.
2 Sigmund Freud and Claude Lévi-Strauss.
3 A phonetic system for transliterating the Chinese language using the Roman alphabet.
4 Steel arch.
5 Lao-tzu.
6 Asgard.
7 A quasi-stellar object; often a powerful source of radio waves.
8 After the Roman general Fabius Maximus Cunctator (the delayer) who defeated stronger opponents by avoiding direct confrontation.
9 Père Joseph (François le Clerc du Tremblay) - a confidant of Cardinal Richelieu, the 'Red Eminence'.
10 The red and blue of Paris and the Bourbon white.
11 The use of contradictory words to create effect, such as 'cruel kindness'.
12 Futurism.
13 In Edinburgh in 1768.
14 Malawi.
15 Grammar, rhetoric and logic.

1 Calliope, Clio, Erato, Euterpe, Melpomene, Polyhmnia, Terpsichore, Thalia, Urania.
2 Ears, noses and throats.
3 Hieronymus Bosch (c1450-1516).
4 In poetry. It is an iambic line comprising 12 syllables, or six feet.
5 Both are derived from activities connected with archery. 'Butts' were shooting ranges, 'fletchers' made arrows.
6 Maori Venture.
7 The Blarney Stone: 'Cormac McCarthy had me built strong in AD 1446'.
8 Uralic.
9 Edward IV.
10 Black and tan.
11 Bertolt Brecht in 1949.
12 Sir Herbert Beerbohm Tree in 1904.
13 Great soul.
14 Literally, a novel with a key. A novel in which real people and real events are depicted in a disguised or semi-disguised way.
15 *Sforzando* - indicating that a strong accent is to be placed on a note or chord.

1 Carbon dioxide, argon, oxygen and nitrogen.
2 22.
3 Yggdrasill and Ymir (also called Aurgelmir).
4 The Nabis, which included Bonnard, Vuillard, and Maillol.
5 The sucre.
6 The won.
7 The Victorian mathematician and scientist Mary Somerville.
8 A nucleus, a coma and a tail.
9 The financier George Hudson, who at one time controlled more than a thousand miles of railway.
10 A plucked string instrument of Graeco-Roman antiquity.
11 500 - 550 million.
12 From 'Tiw', the old English term for the Germanic god of war Tyr, who was identified with the Roman Mars.
13 'The red' - derived from Arabic and probably referring to the colour of the sun-dried bricks of the outer wall of the palace.
14 Dr. Jigoro Kano, in the late 19th century.
15 A type of amphora.

4

1 Parrot fever. The condition is transmitted to humans through a variety of birds.
2 Cro-Magnon man. Cro-Magnon man first appeared about 35,000 years ago. Peking man lived about 500,000 years ago.
3 Hindi, from the word 'pajama' meaning 'drawers'.
4 The Great pyramids at Giza in Egypt, the Hanging Gardens of Babylon, the statue of Zeus at Olympia, the temple of Artemis, the tomb of King Mausolus, the Colossus of Rhodes, and the Pharos of Alexandria.
5 Menelik I.
6 A high conical headdress draped with cloth.
7 Antananarivo.
8 Holocene.
9 A particularly successful greyhound who twice won the English
Greyhound Derby.
10 Ford Madox Brown painted the former, and his grandson Ford Madox Ford wrote the latter.
11 An ant-Tsarist revolt instigated by Russian army officers in December 1825, at the time of the accession of Nicholas I.
12 George II of General Wolfe, after the latter had been criticized.
13 Samarkand.
14 Sir William Walton.
15 Kuo Hsi, who was a Chinese painter and essayist. The others were great Chinese poets.

MIXED BAG **ANSWERS**

1 Barons, Viscounts, Earls, Marquesses, Dukes.
2 Human movement - especially dance.
3 Zoroastrianism.
4 Edward Whymper in 1865.
5 In the playing of flutes and other woodwind instruments.
6 Frisian.
7 *Frigidarium*.
8 Harold Abrahams and Eric Liddell.
9 Sargon of Akkad c2371-2316BC.
10 Phidias.
11 The Niagara Falls.
12 Konstantin Stanislavsky and Vladimir Nemirovich-Danchenko in 1898.
13 The severing of ties between the state and its established church.
14 The Shawnee Indian chief Tecumseh (c1768-1813).
15 Amharic.

1 Sergei Diaghilev, in Paris in 1909.
2 Christopher Brasher and Christopher Chataway.
3 The Jurassic.
4 St. Augustine of Hippo.
5 The Sea of Tranquillity.
6 Removal of the stapes (stirrup) of the middle ear.
7 A horse.
8 The *Victoria*, in the expedition led by Magellan and completed by Elcano (after the former's death en route).
9 George Washington Goethals.
10 Red and white horizontal stripes, with a white star on a blue canton in the top corner.
11 An early Protestant and important disciple of Luther.
12 Vendémiaire (vintage), Brumaire (mist), Frimaire (frost).
13 Dark lines in the solar spectrum.
14 After the punitive Athenian law-giver Draco.
15 A.N. Whitehead.

1 Special lectures delivered periodically to the Royal Society.
2 The unification of Upper and Lower Egypt in c3100 BC.
3 *Destry Rides Again.*
4 Kut is a town in Iraq. The others were ancient Egyptian deities.
5 Napoleon, of Waterloo.
6 The Bell X-1, in 1947.
7 Lord Byron.
8 Bulgaria, from 1908-1918.
9 *The Sentinel*, by Arthur C. Clarke.
10 Hera, Athena, and Aphrodite. The last was deemed most beautiful by Paris.
11 Agamemnon was Clytemnestra's husband and the brother of Menelaus. Menelaus was Helen's husband. Clytemnestra and Helen were sisters.
12 A nomadic Berber people of North Africa.
13 Sirius (or Dog Star) and Canopus.
14 F.W. Murnau.
15 A branch of meteorology concered with clouds.

8

1 Elektron.
2 Bernadotte.
3 Oswald Spengler.
4 Alveoli.
5 Decorative Italian earthenware that is tin-glazed.
6 An ornate galley used by the Doges of Venice on ceremonial occasions.
7 Leopold Stokowski.
8 His lover Kenneth Halliwell.
9 An American songbird, named for its call.
10 Eniwetok Atoll in 1952.
11 Leo Tolstoy.
12 Sir Arthur Quiller-Couch.
13 Auguste Comte.
14 Aachen (Aix-la-Chapelle) - the capital of his western European empire.
15 The Pugwash Conference.

1 Foil, épée and sabre.
2 10101.
3 Louis Botha - from 1910 until his death in 1919.
4 Nikos Kazantzakis.
5 Herstmonceux, Sussex.
6 On the Greek island of Skyros.
7 *Malone Dies*, *Molloy* and *The Unnamable*.
8 Roy Harris.
9 In Venice; it is most famous for presenting music.
10 Rugby, in the play by David Storey.
11 Friedrich Ebert and Field-Marshal von Hindenburg.
12 Utah, Idaho, Montana, South Dakota, Nebraska and Colorado.
13 Bucephalus.
14 The writer and politician Joseph Addison.
15 Michael Checkland, Alasdair Milne, Sir Ian Trethowan.

1 In Greek the letters of *ichthys* (fish) are an acronym of Jesus Christ, Son of God, Saviour.
2 John James Audubon (1785-1851).
3 It is a triangular muscle covering the shoulder prominence.
4 Paul Gauguin.
5 The Kirov Ballet.
6 James I of England (James VI of Scotland).
7 Sir Joseph Paxton.
8 Several members played prominent roles in movements against Ottoman rule in the Balkans.
9 An internationally recognised system for the classification of colours.
10 Ngo Dinh Diem.
11 Sir John Suckling.
12 Henryk Sienkiewicz.
13 San José.
14 Hera, Hermes, Artemis and Athena.
15 They have been carbon dated to c15,000-13,000 BC.

1 Agricola.
2 Those of John Wycliffe.
3 The Tagus - about 620 miles long, followed by the Ebro at about 500 miles.
4 Lloyd's of London.
5 Robert Bolt.
6 Salisbury, Lourenço Marques and Léopoldville.
7 Harrow.
8 A dystopia.
9 An Iron Age people of northern Italy who were superseded by the Etruscans.
10 The forint (equal to 100 fillér) and the dinar (equal to 100 para).
11 Thomas Alva Edison.
12 Abel Tasman.
13 At Dien Bien Phu, in 1954.
14 Hector Hugh Munro.
15 The Augusta National, in Georgia.

12

1 Cronus and Uranus.
2 The Sea of Marmara and the Aegean.
3 The Storting - divided into the Lagting and the Odelsting.
4 The former connects places of the same atmospheric pressure; the latter connects places of the same temperature.
5 Halicarnassus, or modern Bodrum.
6 Robert II, who reigned from 1371-90.
7 Traditional Japanese archery.
8 Edmund Burke.
9 Organisation (formerly Conseil) Européenne pour la Recherche Nucléaire, or The European Organisation for Nuclear Research.
10 His *History of the Peloponnesian War*.
11 Two, three, four, five, seven - not in the same suit.
12 Literally, a disease caused by a doctor. It usually means a disease resulting from treatment.
13 Trinity College, Cambidge.
14 Coventry Cathedral.
15 Hydrogen peroxide.

1 Logarithms.
2 Sir Marc Isambard Brunel (father of Isambard Kingdom Brunel). The tunnel connecting Wapping and Rotherhithe was completed in 1842.
3 Aristotle.
4 Pretoria (administrative), Cape Town (legislative), Bloemfontein (judicial).
5 A plaster preparation used in sculpture, painting and gilding.
6 Brahma, Siva and Vishnu.
7 Chemical messengers which convey nerve impulses.
8 It derives from the Turkish *tulbend* meaning 'turban'.
9 Archon.
10 St. Ignatius of Loyola.
11 The Cheltenham Gold Cup.
12 France in 1764.
13 Dante or Durante Alighieri.
14 Mauna Loa in Hawaii.
15 Czechoslovakia.

1 What are the four main islands of Japan?

2 Which is the longest single span suspension bridge in the world?

3 Which African capital city lies closest to the Equator?

4 What does 'Punjab' mean?

5 In which country is Mount Ararat?

6 What is the name of the city, formerly called Chemnitz?

7 Which republic do the Gilbert Islands form part of?

8 Where is Cape Comorin?

9 What and where is Leptis Magna?

10 Name three of the five autonomous regions of China.

11 What is the most widely spoken Indian language in South America?

12 On which river was ancient Sparta?

13 Where is the Ring of Brogar?

14 Where is the Grande Dixence dam?

15 How does Mali get its name?

1 In which country is the major part of the Kalahari desert?

2 In descending order of size what are the five largest countries?

3 What is the capital of Namibia?

4 Through which counties does the River Severn flow?

5 What is the Hindi name for India?

6 Which country is known to its inhabitants as Suomi?

7 The Flaminian Way ran from Rome to where?

8 Who were the original inhabitants of the island of Pitcairn?

9 What is the state capital of Kansas?

10 In which modern country is the site of the battlefield of Austerlitz?

11 On the ruins of which Aztec capital was Mexico City founded?

12 Where was Kaiser-Wilhelmsland?

13 Where is José Martí International Airport?

14 To which group of islands does Stromboli belong?

15 Into which body of water in the USSR do the Amu Darya and Syr Darya flow?

PLACES QUESTIONS

1 Name the eight counties of Wales.

2 On which planet is the Great Red Spot?

3 Where is the home of the Hopi Indians?

4 In 1945, what divided Korea into two zones?

5 What is the largest lake in the British Isles? ✓

6 What are the five most populous countries - in descending order?

7 Which country is bordered by Togo, Burkina, Niger and Nigeria?

8 Which cities in the Federal Republic of Germany also have the status of Länder (states)?

9 Where in Africa is Venda?

10 What did the ancient Greek and Romans term 'Thule'?

11 With which countries does Austria share its borders?

12 What is the largest Swiss Canton?

13 What are the three most populous cities in Chile?

14 Where is Queen Maud Land?

15 What is the capital of Surinam?

1 Where is the Pirelli skyscraper?

2 Where is Machu Picchu?

3 Which island in the Netherlands Antilles gives its name to a famous liqueur?

4 What is the deepest freshwater lake?

5 Where and what exactly is Maelstrom?

6 What is the capital of the People's Republic of Mongolia?

7 What does the Gutenberg Discontinuity separate?

8 Name three of the seven United Arab Emirates.

9 How many union republics constitute the USSR?

10 What are the New Hebrides called now?

11 In which town is William the Conqueror buried?

12 Which towns were known as 'Gades' and 'Hispalis' to the Romans?

13 What is the largest city on Tahiti island?

14 Which is the world's longest man-made waterway?

15 What is the Curzon Line?

1 What was Pangea and which land masses did it break apart to form?

2 How do the Canaries get their name?

3 What was the Forbidden City of Tibet?

4 On which mountain are the massive heads of four American Presidents carved?

5 When was the Eiffel Tower built?

6 Where are the Aleutian Islands?

7 Which town was struck by this century's most lethal earthquake?

8 Which is the largest lake in Hungary?

9 Where is the Fergana Basin?

10 How long is the coastline of the Philippines?
a) 4,642 miles b) 8,052 miles c) 30,602 miles d) 45,908 miles

11 What is a 'polder'?

12 What is the name of the strait between Victoria and Tasmania?

13 What does 'Thailand' mean?

14 What is the capital of Niger?

15 Which islands were once called the 'Sandwich Islands'?

1 Which two towns were linked by the first commerical railway?

2 Which river ran through Babylon?

3 With how many countries does Lesotho share its border?

4 For which product is the town of Meissen famous?

5 For what are the cities of Ife and Benin both renowned?

6 In which countries are the Angel and Tugela Falls?

7 What are the four largest islands in the world?

8 What is the French name for Lake Geneva?

9 For what is Ngorongoro national park renowned?

10 Which is the most populous Soviet city east of the Urals?

11 What does 'Yugoslav' mean?

12 Where are the Doldrums?

13 Which were the seven Anglo-Saxon kingdoms known as the Heptarchy?

14 How does New York get its name?

15 What are the three largest ethnic groups in Nigeria?

1 In geological terms what are the earth's four youngest mountain ranges?

2 What does 'Soweto' stand for?

3 Of which country are Ghegs and Tosks the principal ethnic groups?

4 How many moons has Mars got, and what are their names?

5 What is the largest monolith in the world?

6 What is the most westerly point of continental Europe?

7 In which gulf is the island of Salamis?

8 Where are the Mendip Hills?

9 Which was the first London University college to be founded and when?

10 Where in North America is L'Anse aux Meadows and why is it important?

11 Where did the Nok civilization flourish?

12 Which Icelandic volcano was known as 'The Mountain of Hell'?

13 What is the highest mountain in the USSR?

14 Which three countries does Borneo belong to?

15 Where is the Bay of Fundy?

1 Where are the Western and Eastern Ghats?

2 In which town is the Royal Mint?

3 What are the two largest minor planets?

4 When did South Africa leave the Commonwealth?

5 Of which ancient empire was Hattushash the capital?

6 What is Euzkadi?

7 Which was the first city to be founded in the New World?

8 In which state is Camp David retreat?

9 On which river is the city of Mandalay?

10 Name the nine major planets in order of increasing mean distance from the sun.

11 Which is the most southerly capital city?

12 What are the two highest mountains in the Alps?

13 Where is the Denmark Strait?

14 In which mountain range is K2?

15 What is the English name for the constellation Mensa?

1 At the junction of which two rivers is Belgrade situated?

2 Where and what is the 'Ka'bah'?

3 Which Cambridge college was founded in the late 1970s?

4 What does Tokyo mean, and what was its former name?

5 Name the six federated republics of Yugoslavia?

6 Of which African country was Gondar once the capital?

7 What is the longest glacier?

8 Where exactly did Stanley find Livingstone?

9 Where does the Harmattan wind blow?

10 Which is the deepest point on the earth's surface?

11 Why is the island of Elephanta famous?

12 In which constellation is the Horsehead nebula?

13 Where is the Aozou strip?

14 How do geysers get their name?

15 Which Roman province did you enter by crossing the Rubicon northwards?

1 Which language of Europe is Semitic?

2 How does Mount Kosciusko - Australia's highest peak - get its name?

3 How does China's Yellow River get its name?

4 Who designed Coventry Cathedral?

5 What are the two longest rivers in Europe?

6 What is the capital of Greenland?

7 What is the capital of Burundi?

8 Where is the Mount Wilson Observatory?

9 What are the two main islands of Fiji?

10 What and where is the Shwe Dagon?

11 How does the Italian town of Alessandria get its name?

12 What was the ancient name for the Dardanelles?

13 What is the English name for the constellation Monoceros?

14 What is the name of the desert that occupies southern Saudi Arabia and parts of Yemen, S. Yemen, Oman and the United Arab Emirates?

15 Where are the headquarters of UNESCO?

1 Which river flows through Florence?

2 Which country has the largest Muslim population?

3 How does the volcanic island of Surtsey get its name?

4 To which country do the Galapagos Islands belong?

5 At the junction of which two rivers do Argentina, Brazil and Paraguay meet?

6 In which constellation is Spica?

7 For uncovering evidence of which civilization was Arthur Evans knighted in 1911?

8 How did Natal get its name?

9 Name four of the Seven Hills of Rome?

10 Which country is the world's main supplier of teak?

11 What is the principal crop of the United Arab Emirates?

12 Where is the port of Balikpapan?

13 What is the Cassini division?

14 What is the Pope's cathedral church?

15 To which language grouping do Kurdish and Pashto belong?

1 What is the currency of Austria?

2 For what is the Italian town of Carrara world famous?

3 Name the Great Lakes.

4 What was 'great, grey-green greasy'?

5 Describe the Syrian flag.

6 Where is O'Hare airport?

7 Which country is divided into the Oesling and the Bon Pays?

8 Where and what is the Hill of Tara?

9 In which church is Napoleon's tomb?

10 Through which countries does the Brahmaputra flow?

11 What was the language of the Aztecs?

12 Which four regions of Spain border on France?

13 Name the Inns of Court.

14 Where is Schloss Schönbrunn and why was it built?

15 Who first established a permanent Dutch settlement in South Africa?

1 Which rivers separate Germany from Poland?

2 In which county is the Giant's Causeway?

3 What is an 'oblast'?

4 To which reformer is Eros in Piccadilly a tribute?

5 In which county is Tolpuddle?

6 What were the two previous names of Volgograd?

7 Who are the aboriginal inhabitants of Japan?

8 Of which Canadian province is *parva sub ingenti* (the small under the protection of the great) the motto?

9 Which mountain in Greece has been forbidden to women since the eleventh century?

10 In which country are the Kaieteur Falls and by which river are they formed?

11 What is the least densely populated country of Asia?

12 Which planet has satellites that include Miranda, Ariel and Titania?

13 What were the two great cities of the Indus Valley civilization?

14 Where and what is Angkor Wat?

15 In which country is the town of Fray Bentos?

PLACES **ANSWERS**

1 Honshu, Kyushu, Hokkaido, Shikoku.
2 The Humber Bridge.
3 Kampala.
4 Five-rivers. It refers to five tributaries of the Indus.
5 Turkey.
6 Karl-Marx-Stadt, in E. Germany.
7 Kiribati.
8 At the most southern point of India.
9 An ancient Carthaginian and Roman city in Libya which is now a site of outstanding classical ruins.
10 Inner Mongolia, Kwangsi, Ningsia, Sinkiang, Tibet.
11 Quechua.
12 The Eurotas.
13 It is a megalith in Orkney.
14 In Switzerland on the River Dixence.
15 After the Mali empire that flourished in West Africa during the Middle Ages.

1 Botswana.
2 USSR, Canada, China, USA, Brazil.
3 Windhoek.
4 Powys, Shropshire, Hereford and Worcester, Gloucestershire.
5 Bharat.
6 Finland.
7 Rimini (Ariminum).
8 The mutineers from the Bounty.
9 Topeka.
10 Czechoslovakia.
11 Tenochtitlán.
12 The north-eastern part of New Guinea - a German colony until 1914.
13 Havana, Cuba.
14 Lipari Islands (Isole Eolie).
15 The Aral Sea.

PLACES ANSWERS

1 Clwyd, Dyfed, Gwent, Gwynedd, Mid Glamorgan, Powys, S. Glamorgan, W. Glamorgan.
2 It is an atmospheric or meteorological phenomenon appearing as an oval mark on the planet Jupiter.
3 North-eastern Arizona.
4 The 38th parallel.
5 Lough Neagh in Northern Ireland.
6 China, India, USSR, USA, Indonesia.
7 Benin.
8 West Berlin, Hamburg, and Bremen (including Bremerhaven).
9 It is a Homeland in South Africa, proclaimed an independent republic in 1979.
10 The most northerly land in the world that they knew of.
11 W. Germany, Czechoslovakia, Hungary, Yugoslavia, Italy, Switzerland (and Liechtenstein).
12 Graubünden (Grisons).
13 Santiago, Valparaíso, Concepción.
14 In Antarctica - representing the major Norwegian claim.
15 Paramaribo.

1 Milan.
2 It is an Inca site in Peru.
3 Curaçao.
4 Lake Baikal in the USSR.
5 It is the name of a strait and its perilous current between two of the Lofoten islands of Norway.
6 Ulaanbaatar.
7 The earth's mantle from the core.
8 Abu Dhabi, Dubai, Ajman, Sharjah, Umm al-Qaiwain, Ras al-Khaimah and Fujairah.
9 15.
10 Vanuatu - since independence in 1980.
11 Caen in Normandy.
12 Cadiz and Seville.
13 Papeete, the capital of French Polynesia.
14 The Grand Canal in China, extending approximately 1000 miles from Peking to Hang-chou.
15 A line between Poland and Russia, proposed in 1920 and named after the foreign minister Lord Curzon, which was accepted by the two countries as their border in 1945.

1 The hypothetical supercontinent that, according to the theory of continental drift, broke apart to form Laurasia and Gondwanaland, which in turn formed the present continents.

2 From the Latin *canis* meaning 'dog'. The islands were named after the wild dogs that roamed there.

3 Lhasa.

4 Mount Rushmore.

5 1887 - 1889 for the Paris exhibition and celebrating the hundredth anniversary of the French Revolution.

6 In the north Pacific Ocean forming the southern perimeter of the Bering Sea.

7 Tangshan in eastern China in 1976. Mortality estimates vary between 242,000 and 750,000.

8 Balaton.

9 In the USSR, near the Chinese and Afghan borders.

10 8,052 miles.

11 A tract of land that has been reclaimed from the sea, or other body of water - particularly in the Netherlands.

12 The Bass Strait.

13 Land of the free.

14 Niamey.

15 The islands of Hawaii.

6

1 Stockton and Darlington.

2 The Euphrates.

3 One. It is surrounded by South Africa.

4 Porcelain.

5 African art.

6 Venezuela and South Africa.

7 Australia (if not considered a continent), Greenland, New Guinea, Borneo and Madagascar.

8 Lac Léman.

9 It contains a massive extinct volcanic crater filled with game.

10 Tashkent.

11 Southern Slav.

12 They are calm regions of the oceans near the Equator.

13 Kent, Essex, Sussex, Wessex, E. Anglia, Mercia, Northumbria.

14 After the Duke of York - later James II.

15 The Hausa, Yoruba and Ibo.

PLACES ANSWERS

1 Himalayas, Alps, Pyrenees, Zagros.
2 South-western townships.
3 Albania.
4 Two. Phobos and Deimos.
5 Ayers Rock in Australia.
6 Cape Roca.
7 The Saronic Gulf in the Aegean Sea.
8 In Somerset, extending to Avon.
9 University College - founded in 1826 as the University of London.
10 In Newfoundland. It is the site of Viking remains.
11 In what is now central Nigeria - from about 500 BC to AD 200.
12 Hekla.
13 Pik Kommunizma (24, 590 feet).
14 Sarawak and Sabah to Malaysia, Kalimantan to Indonesia,and Brunei.
15 Between Nova Scotia and New Brunswick, Canada.

1 In India. They are mountain ranges along the western and eastern coasts.
2 Llantrisant, Wales.
3 Ceres is the largest, Pallas is the second largest.
4 1961.
5 The Hittite.
6 It is the Basque term for the Basque Country.
7 Isabela - in the present day Dominican Republic.
8 Maryland.
9 The Irrawaddy.
10 Mercury, Venus, Earth, Mars, Jupiter, Saturn, Uranus, Neptune and Pluto.
11 Wellington.
12 Mont Blanc, Monte Rosa.
13 Between Greenland and Iceland.
14 The Karakoram.
15 The Table Mountain.

1 The Danube and Sava.
2 It is the shrine in the courtyard of the Great Mosque at Mecca containing the Black Stone.
3 Robinson College.
4 'Eastern capital'. It was formerly called Edo.
5 Serbia, Croatia, Slovenia, Bosnia and Herzegovina, Macedonia and Montenegro.
6 Ethiopia, from 1632-1855.
7 The Lambert glacier.
8 At Ujiji, on Lake Tanganyika.
9 South-west from the Sahara across W. Africa to the Atlantic.
10 Challenger Deep in Marianas Trench, in the W. Pacific - approximately 36,000 feet deep.
11 For its cave temples dedicated to Hindu gods.
12 Orion.
13 In Chad, along its border with Libya.
14 After Geysir - a geyser in Iceland whose name means 'to rush forth or rage'.
15 Cisalpine Gaul.

1 Maltese.
2 After the Polish nationalist and patriot Tadeusz Kosciuszko (1746-1817).
3 From the amount of sediment it carries.
4 Sir Basil Spence.
5 The Volga followed by the Danube.
6 Godthåb.
7 Bujumbura.
8 Just outside Pasadena, California.
9 Viti Levu and Vanua Levu.
10 A Buddhist pagoda on the outskirts of Rangoon in Burma.
11 After its founder Pope Alexander III.
12 The Hellespont.
13 The Unicorn.
14 Rub al-Khali.
15 Paris.

1 The Arno.
2 Indonesia.
3 After the Norse god of fire - Surt.
4 Ecuador.
5 The Paraná and the Iguaçú.
6 It was the brightest star in Virgo.
7 Minoan Crete.
8 It was sighted by Vasco da Gama on Christmas day and named Terra Natalis.
9 Capitoline, Quirinal, Viminal, Esquiline, Caelian, Aventine, Palatine.
10 Burma.
11 Dates.
12 On the south-east coast of the island of Borneo.
13 A division in the ring system of Saturn.
14 The Basilica of St John Lateran.
15 Iranian.

1 The schilling - comprising 100 groschen.
2 Marble.
3 Lakes Superior, Michigan, Huron, Erie, Ontario.
4 The Limpopo - according to Kipling.
5 Three horizontal bands of red, white and black with two green stars on the white band.
6 Chicago.
7 Luxembourg.
8 A hill in County Meath, Eire. It was the seat of Irish kings until the 6th century AD and contains a number of ancient monuments.
9 Dôme des Invalides, Paris.
10 China (Tibet), India and Bangladesh.
11 Nahuatl.
12 Basque country, Navarre, Aragon and Catalonia.
13 Lincoln's Inn, Gray's Inn, Inner Temple, Middle Temple.
14 Vienna. It was built as the summer palace of the Habsburgs.
15 Jan van Riebeeck, in 1652 - at Capetown - for the Dutch East India Company.

1 The Oder and Neisse.
2 County Antrim.
3 A territorial and administrative region in the USSR.
4 The 7th Earl of Shaftesbury.
5 Dorset.
6 Tsaritsyn and Stalingrad.
7 The Ainu.
8 Prince Edward Island, the smallest Canadian province.
9 Mount Athos (or Holy Mountain) in northern Greece.
10 In Guyana - formed by the River Potaro.
11 Mongolia.
12 Uranus.
13 Harappa and Mohenjo-Daro.
14 A temple complex in Cambodia.
15 Uruguay.

1 In Greek mythology, what was the Chimaera?

2 Who says: "He is the very pineapple of politeness"?

3 What did the poet André Breton define as 'pure psychic automatism'?

4 Who used the narrator Marlow?

5 Name the three main characters in Joyce's *Ulysses*.

6 What was the true identity of Baron Corvo?

7 Which novels comprise *The Raj Quartet*?

8 Which husband and wife founded the Hogarth Press?

9 Whose self-composed epitaph was "Here lies one whose name was writ in water"?

10 An illiterate herdsman, he has been called the first English Christian poet. Who?

11 How many plays by Sophocles have survived?

12 In the Old Testament who says ironically "Let us eat and drink; for tomorrow we shall die"?

13 Name the four novels by Nathaniel West.

14 The *Epic of Gilgamesh* is inscribed on 12 incomplete tablets which were found in the library of King Ashurbanipal of Assyria. In which language is it written?

15 Who wrote: "The ghost of Roger Casement is beating on the door"?

WORDS QUESTIONS

1 What does the name 'Oedipus' mean?

2 In which T.S. Eliot play do the mythical Eumenides (Furies) appear?

3 Who wrote *The New Machiavelli*?

4 Who concluded: "Cogito ergo sum"?

5 Who wrote: "I fear the Greeks even when they bring gifts"?

6 What are the three scripts that appear on the Rosetta Stone?

7 Which Shakespeare play is set in Vienna?

8 Who wrote: "To err is human, to forgive divine"?

9 Who wrote the autobiographical volumes *Changing* and *Choices*?

10 What is subtitled 'A Comedy and a Philosophy'?

11 What is the origin of the word 'trivial'?

12 Who is Grahame Greene's 'burnt-out case'?

13 Which doesn't belong and why: Pride, Melancholy, Indolence, Psyche?

14 What is the motto of the Order of the Thistle?

15 Who wrote *The Physiology of Taste* ("Physiologie du goût")?

1 What consists of 100 stories told by ten young people fleeing the plague?

2 Crippled at Lepanto, he was captured by pirates and became a slave. Which writer?

3 Who created Svengali?

4 Who said: "I am but mad north-north-west"?

5 Who wrote *All Quiet on the Western Front*?

6 Who is generally regarded as the greatest Portuguese poet?

7 From what is the word 'dunce' derived?

8 Who won the 1984 and 1985 Nobel prizes for literature?

9 Which novel begins with the end of a sentence left unfinished on the last page?

10 Who wrote, and of whom: "All he did was to remember like the old and be honest like children"?

11 What are the names of the two tramps in *Waiting for Godot*?

12 Who called philosophy "That great mother of the sciences"?

13 Who wrote the play *Anne of the Thousand Days*?

14 What name is given to a song or poem in honour of the god Dionysus?

15 In which novel did the secret agent George Smiley first appear?

1 Name the five novels by Scott Fitzgerald?

2 What did John Milton call "Mother of arts and eloquence"?

3 Of whom did Coleridge say: "To see him act, is like reading Shakespeare by flashes of lightning"?

4 Which novel first mentioned Ruritania?

5 Who wrote *The Autobiography of a Super-Tramp*?

6 In which language was *Darkness at Noon* written?

7 What are Charles Dickens' two historical novels?

8 Who wrote *The Golden Ass*?

9 In which year did the National Theatre open on its present site?

10 Who wrote *The Bridge of San Luis Rey*?

11 Who was Lewis Baboon?

12 The sonnet *The New Colossus* is carved on the Statue of Liberty. Who wrote it?

13 Who is regarded as the founder of Greek scepticism?

14 Who wrote *The Four Zoas*?

15 Which poet did Byron call "Nature's sternest painter, yet her best"?

1 Who survived the sinking of the *Pequod*?

2 What is Goncharov's best known work?

3 Which significant English poet died aged 17?

4 Who wrote the novels *Tancred* and *Vivien Grey*?

5 In the Authorized Version of the Bible, what are the two last books of the Old Testament?

6 What is the literal meaning of 'Beelzebub'?

7 Who wrote the philosophical works *Either - Or* and *Fear and Trembling*?

8 Which poet wrote the screenplay for Carné's film *Les Enfants du Paradis*.

9 Link the following: Philoctetes, Paris, Achilles and Memnon.

10 According to Aristotle, something "is the best provision for old age". What?

11 Who says: "When the mind's free the body's delicate"?

12 Which English poet was knighted in 1979?

13 Who wrote *A Dissertation on Roast Pig* and *A Chapter on Ears*?

14 What was "little more than the crimes, follies, and misfortunes of mankind"?

15 Name the two writers associated with the development of the 'cut-up and fold-in' literary technique.

1 Who created the character Pinocchio?

2 Which John Steinbeck novel was based on the story of Cain and Abel?

3 Who wrote *The Battle of the Books*?

4 Who was a monk and a doctor but is better known for writing about giants?

5 Who created the system on which 'method acting' is based?

6 Who wrote *Erec et Enide*?

7 Who said a house should be a 'machine for living in'?

8 Of which famous love affair did Alexander Pope and George Moore both write?

9 Who wrote *Charley's Aunt*?

10 Who said: "A cucumber should be well-sliced, dressed with pepper and vinegar and then thrown out"?

11 What was *Sturm und Drang*?

12 How many lines are there in a Spenserian stanza?

13 Whom did Sherlock Holmes consider to be his master in the art of deduction?

14 In *The Canterbury Tales*, who relates the 'Tale of Melibeus'?

15 In which play does Dr Stockman remark: "our civil community is founded on the pestiferous soil of falsehood"?

1 Which was the only book published by the philosopher Wittgenstein in his lifetime?

2 Who wrote *The King of Schnorrers*?

3 Which three Dubliners won the Nobel Prize for literature?

4 Who is the subject of Tennyson's *In Memoriam*?

5 Who wrote *The Long and the Short and the Tall*?

6 What is a spondee?

7 Who wrote *A Satyr against Mankind*?

8 In Homer's Odyssey, who detained Odysseus for seven years on the island of Ogygia?

9 Where would you find Yoknapatawpha?

10 How is *Les Plaideurs* unique among the plays of Racine?

11 Which one name did Shakespeare use five times for different characters, and in which plays do the characters appear?

12 How does the second verse of the National Anthem begin?

13 Who described his relationship with Madame de Staël in the novel *Adolphe*?

14 Who wrote *Modern Science and Anarchism*?

15 What was Conrad's first novel?

1 What was Thomas Hardy's last novel?

2 In Greek myth, of which realm was Pygmalion king?

3 Who won the Booker Prize in 1984, 1985 and 1986?

4 Who wrote *The Subjection of Women* (1869)?

5 How did the poet Shelley die?

6 What were the Playboy Riots?

7 Which work by Edward Bond became the final play to be banned by the Lord Chamberlain?

8 What was the previous name of the Royal Shakespeare Theatre?

9 What is the origin of the word 'dinosaur'?

10 Who created the detective C. Auguste Dupin?

11 Who wrote: "The road of excess leads to the palace of wisdom"?

12 Which novel begins: "The family of Dashwood had been long settled in Sussex"?

13 What is the name of the villain in *The Hunchback of Nôtre Dame*?

14 Which Sartre play is set in hell?

15 Who are 'the unacknowledged legislators of the world'?

1 Who created the character Peregrine Pickle?

2 What do the authors of *Equus* and *Sleuth* have in common?

3 Who wrote *Le Bâteau Ivre*?

4 Who is generally assumed to have written *Piers Plowman*?

5 Which of Shakespeare's plays was supposedly written in collaboration with John Fletcher?

6 Who was "Alone, alone, all, all alone"?

7 Which plays comprise the 'Oresteia Trilogy' by Aeschylus?

8 Which rhyme scheme is used in Dante's *Divine Comedy*?

9 Who stated: "Property is theft"?

10 Which was the only book of poems by Sylvia Plath to be published before her suicide?

11 Who said: "messages are for Western Union"?

12 In which novel did Hercule Poirot make his first appearance?

13 Who wrote an autobiography entitled *Words*?

14 Who said: "I wouldn't put it past God to arrange a virgin birth if he wanted, but I very much doubt if he would because it seems contrary to the way he deals with persons"?

15 Which philosopher did Dr Johnson describe as "a very bad man"?

1 Who says "my mistress with the monster is in love"?

2 What name is given to the sequence of novels in which Natty Bumppo appears under various names?

3 Who wrote *Eminent Victorians*?

4 Who said: "Another such victory and we are done for"?

5 Which philosopher wrote the self-interpretive work *Ecce Homo* (Behold the Man)?

6 Which Sicilian won the 1934 Nobel Prize for literature?

7 Which school of philosophy did Zeno of Citium found?

8 What is the name of Molière's Miser?

9 Which American writer used the pen name H.D.?

10 Which novelist coined the term 'nihilist'?

11 Who founded *The Times* and what was its original name?

12 Which novel did Fielding burlesque in *Joseph Andrews*?

13 Who wrote: "Nature I loved, and, next to nature art"?

14 Who wrote nearly 2,000 poems of which only seven were published in her lifetime?

15 Who wrote of "Nature ... vanquished by art"?

1 What is the origin of the word 'chauvinist'?

2 Which of the following was not a poet laureate: Wordsworth, Pope, Tennyson, Dryden, Bridges?

3 Who wrote the novel *Gigi*?

4 What do the authors of *Beowulf* and *Sir Gawain and the Green Knight* have in common?

5 What was the first labour of Hercules?

6 What was Horace's full Latin name?

7 Who originated the theory of the 'Theatre of Cruelty'?

8 Who wrote *The Spanish Tragedy*?

9 Which play begins 'If you shall chance, Camillo, to visit Bohemia'?

10 In mythology, who wielded Mjollnir?

11 What is the name of Marlowe's Jew of Malta?

12 'No bishop, no king.': Whose dictum?

13 Who wrote *A Day in the Death of Joe Egg*?

14 Which Hemingway novel was recently published for the first time?

15 Who is the gamekeeper in *Lady Chatterley's Lover*?

1 How does the crane called a 'derrick' gets its name?

2 Who wrote the novel *Gentlemen Prefer Blondes*?

3 Who wrote *Common Sense, Public Good* and *The Age of Reason*?

4 Who is 'Our Mutual Friend'?

5 Who wrote the poem *A Dream of Gerontius*?

6 What is the full title of the novel *Vanity Fair*?

7 Which novel by Horace Walpole is considered to be the first gothic novel?

8 Which dramatist was allegedly killed by a tortoise?

9 Which poet won four Pulitzer prizes between 1924 and 1943?

10 Who said: 'I was never an Angry Young Man'?

11 For what achievement is Saint Jerome best known?

12 Who wrote the play *The Quare Fellow*?

13 Who wrote *Voyna i mir*?

14 Who wrote *The Casuarina Tree*?

15 Who wrote 'For an old bitch gone in the teeth, For a botched civilization'?

1 Who founded *Scrutiny* magazine?

2 Who wrote *The Heart of the Antarctic* and *South*?

3 What were Goethe's last words?

4 Which playwright accused Winston Churchill of being involved in causing the death of the Polish General Sikorski?

5 Who wrote the novels *Planet of the Apes* and *The Bridge on the River Kwai*?

6 Military engineer, convict, soldier, epileptic, gambler, writer. Who?

7 How did Voltaire sum up the Holy Roman Empire?

8 In which novel do Castorp, Naphta and Settembrini appear?

9 Which poem begins 'A thing of beauty is a joy forever'?

10 Who wrote *The Heart is a Lonely Hunter*?

11 Who created the character Raffles?

12 In which story did Sherlock Holmes first appear?

13 Which Bulgarian/British novelist won the Nobel Prize in 1981?

14 For what is the 19th century writer Edward Fitzgerald cheifly remembered?

15 Who wrote the play *Ubu Roi*?

WORDS ANSWERS

1 A monster with a lion's head, a goat's body and a serpent's tail.
2 Mrs. Malaprop in Sheridan's *The Rivals*.
3 Surrealism, in the *Manifesto of Surrealism* (1924).
4 Joseph Conrad, in various novels.
5 Leopold Bloom, Molly Bloom, Stephen Dedalus.
6 The novelist **Frederick William Rolfe**.
7 *The Jewel in the Crown*, *The Day of the Scorpion*, *The Towers of Silence* and *A Division of the Spoils*.
8 Virginia and Leonard Woolf in 1917.
9 John Keats.
10 Caedmon.
11 Seven (and some fragments), out of over 100 written.
12 Isaiah.
13 *The Dream Life of Balso Snell*, *Miss Lonelyhearts*, 'A Cool Million', 'The Day of the Locust'.
14 Akkadian.
15 W.B. Yeats, in *The Ghost of Roger Casement*.

2

1 Swell-Foot.
2 *The Family Reunion*.
3 H.G. Wells.
4 René Descartes.
5 Virgil, in the *Aeneid*.
6 Egyptian hieroglyphic and demotic, and Greek.
7 *Measure for Measure*.
8 Alexander Pope in "An Essay on Criticism".
9 The actress, Liv Ullman.
10 G.B. Shaw's *Man and Superman*.
11 From the Latin *trivium* meaning the junction of three roads.
12 The architect, Querry.
13 Pride. Keats wrote odes 'to' or 'on' the last three.
14 'No one provokes me with impunity'.
15 Anthelme Brillat-Savarin.

1 Boccaccio's *The Decameron*.
2 Miguel de Cervantes.
3 George du Maurier in the novel *Trilby*.
4 Shakespeare's Hamlet.
5 Erich Maria Remarque.
6 Luis de Camoes.
7 The name of the 13th-century philospher John Duns Scotus.
8 The Czech poet Jaroslav Seifert in 1984, and the French novelist Claude Simon in 1985.
9 Joyce's *Finnegan's Wake*.
10 W.H. Auden on S. Freud in the poem *In Memory of Sigmund Freud*.
11 Vladimir and Estragon.
12 Francis Bacon.
13 Maxwell Anderson.
14 A dithyramb.
15 *Call for the Dead* by John le Carré.

4

1 *This Side of Paradise, The Beautiful and Damned, The Great Gatsby, Tender is the Night*, and *The Last Tycoon*.
2 Athens.
3 Edmund Kean.
4 *The Prisoner of Zenda*, by Anthony Hope.
5 W.H. Davies.
6 German.
7 *A Tale of Two Cities*, and *Barnaby Rudge*.
8 Lucius Apuleius.
9 1976.
10 Thornton Wilder.
11 The character representing the French King and the French nation in John Arbuthnot's *The History of John Bull*.
12 Emma Lazarus.
13 Pyrrho of Elis (c360-272 BC)
14 William Blake.
15 George Crabbe.

WORDS ANSWERS

1 Ishmael, the narrator of *Moby Dick*.
2 *Oblomov*.
3 Thomas Chatterton (1752-70).
4 Benjamin Disraeli.
5 'Zechariah' and 'Malachi'.
6 'Lord of the Flies', it is derived from Hebrew.
7 Soren Kierkegaard.
8 Jacques Prévert.
9 Philoctetes killed Paris who killed Achilles who killed Memnon.
10 Education.
11 King Lear.
12 William Empson.
13 Charles Lamb.
14 History - according to Edward Gibbon.
15 William Burroughs and Brion Gysin.

1 Collodi.
2 *East of Eden*.
3 Jonathan Swift.
4 François Rabelais - the 16th century author of *Gargantua* and *Pantagruel*.
5 Konstantin Stanislavsky.
6 Chrétien de Troyes.
7 The architect Le Corbusier.
8 That of Abélard and Héloise.
9 Brandon Thomas.
10 Dr Johnson.
11 It literally means 'storm and stress', and refers to the German literary movement that preceded Romanticism, taking its name from the title of a play by M. Klinger.
12 9
13 His brother Mycroft.
14 Chaucer himself.
15 *An Enemy of the People*, by Henrik Ibsen.

1 *Tractatus logico-philosophicus.*
2 Israel Zangwill.
3 W.B. Yeats, G.B. Shaw and Samuel Beckett.
4 Arthur Henry Hallam.
5 Willis Hall.
6 A metrical foot consisting of two long or stressed syllables.
7 John Wilmot, 2nd Earl of Rochester.
8 Calypso.
9 It is a fictional region in the novels of William Faulkner.
10 It is his only comedy.
11 Antonio. *Much Ado About Nothing. The Tempest. Two Gentlemen of Verona. The Merchant of Venice. Twelfth Night.*
12 'O Lord our God arise, Scatter her enemies,And make them fall.'
13 Benjamin Constant.
14 Prince Peter Alexeivich Kropotkin.
15 'Almayer's Folly' (1895).

1 *Jude the Obscure* (1896).
2 Cyprus.
3 Anita Brookner, Keri Hulme, Kingsley Amis.
4 John Stuart Mill.
5 He drowned.
6 Riots at the first performance of J.M. Synge's *Playboy of the Western World* in Dublin in 1907.
7 *Early Morning* in 1968.
8 The Shakespeare Memorial Theatre.
9 From the Greek meaning 'terrible lizard'.
10 Edgar Allan Poe.
11 William Blake, in *Proverbs of Hell.*
12 *Sense and Sensibility*, by Jane Austen.
13 Claude Frollo.
14 'Huis-clos' (also known as 'In Camera').
15 The poets - according to Shelley.

1 Tobias Smollett.
2 Peter Shaffer wrote *Equus* and his brother Anthony wrote *Sleuth*.
3 Arthur Rimbaud.
4 William Langland.
5 *Henry VIII*. (They are also thought to have co-written *The Two Noble Kinsmen*).
6 Coleridge's Ancient Mariner.
7 *Agamemnon, The Libation-Bearers* and *Eumenides*.
8 'Terza rima' - The second line of each group of three lines rhymes with the first and third of the next group of three lines: aba, bcb, cdc, ded.
9 Pierre-Joseph Proudhon in *What is Property*.
10 *The Colossus* (1960).
11 Sam Goldwyn.
12 *The Mysterious Affair at Styles* (1920).
13 Jean-Paul Sartre.
14 Rt. Rev. David Jenkins, Bishop of Durham.
15 Jean-Jacques Rousseau.

1 Puck in *A Midsummer Night's Dream*.
2 *Leather Stocking Tales* by James Fenimore Cooper.
3 Lytton Strachey.
4 King Pyrrhus of Epirus.
5 Friedrich Nietzsche.
6 Luigi Pirandello.
7 The Stoic.
8 Harpagon.
9 Hilda Doolittle.
10 Ivan Sergeyevich Turgenev.
11 John Walter. It first appeared in 1785 as the *Daily Universal Register*.
12 *Pamela* by Samuel Richardson.
13 Walter Savage Landor.
14 Emily Dickinson.
15 Michelangelo, in one of his sonnets.

1 It is derived from Nicolas Chauvin - a soldier who was devoted to Napoleon and military glory.
2 Pope.
3 Colette.
4 They are unknown.
5 The killing of the Nemean Lion.
6 Quintus Horatius Flaccus.
7 Antonin Artaud.
8 Thomas Kyd.
9 *The Winter's Tale.*
10 Thor - it was his hammer.
11 Barabas.
12 James I of England (James VI of Scotland).
13 Peter Nichols.
14 *The Garden of Eden.*
15 Mellors.

12

1 After Derrick - a celebrated Tyburn hangman.
2 Anita Loos.
3 Thomas Paine.
4 John Harmon.
5 Cardinal J.H. Newman.
6 *Vanity Fair, a Novel without a Hero.*
7 *The Castle of Otranto* (1764).
8 Aeschylus. It was dropped on to his head by an eagle.
9 Robert Frost.
10 Kingsley Amis.
11 The Vulgate - the translation of the Bible into Latin.
12 Brendan Behan.
13 Tolstoy - it is the Russian name for *War and Peace.*
14 Somerset Maugham.
15 Ezra Pound in *Hugh Selwyn Mauberley.*

1 F.R. Leavis and his wife Q.D. Leavis.
2 Sir Ernest Shackleton.
3 'More light!'
4 Rolf Hochhuth in *Soldiers*.
5 Pierre Boulle.
6 Fyodor Dostoyevsky.
7 He said it was 'neither holy, nor Roman nor an empire'.
8 Thomas Mann's *The Magic Mountain*.
9 Keats's *Endymion*.
10 Carson McCullers.
11 E.W. Hornung.
12 *A Study in Scarlet*.
13 Elias Canetti.
14 His translation of *The Rubaiyat of Omar Khayyam*.
15 Alfred Jarry.

1 Who composed the music to the film *On the Waterfront*?

2 Which instrument was formerly known as a sackbut?

3 Who composed the music to *Deutschland Über Alles*?

4 Who was the first singer to sell a million copies of a record?

5 Name the first three tracks on the Beatles' *Sgt. Pepper* album?

6 Who composed a set of twelve piano pieces entitled *Iberia*?

7 Which composer was known as the 'Austrian Napoleon'?

8 Whom did Fats Waller describe as "God"?

9 For whom was Verdi's *Requiem* composed?

10 Who wrote the libretto for Richard Strauss's *Der Rosenkavalier*?

11 For which musician did Mozart write his clarinet concerto?

12 In which keys are the four symphonies by Brahms?

13 Which group recorded Motown Records' first million seller?

14 Who wrote the opera *Mozart and Salieri* in 1897?

15 Who commissioned *Rhapsody in Blue* and conducted its first performance?

1 Who wrote *Fascinating Rhythm*, who wrote *My Funny Valentine* and who wrote *Tea for Two*?

2 What was the sequel to *The Beggar's Opera*?

3 Name two of the Rolling Stones' first three single releases, and the composer of one of them.

4 Who composed the *Bachianas Brasileiras*?

5 What was Billie Holiday's real name?

6 Which Charles Chaplin composition topped the charts in 1967?

7 Which work by Thomas Tallis is written for 40 parts for 8 5-voice choirs?

8 Name Benjamin Britten's two collaborators for the opera *Billy Budd*?

9 Who promised an eighth symphony to Sir Thomas Beecham and others - but never delivered?

10 What was the Beatles' last no. 1 single in the UK?

11 Which man helped develop the careers of Bessie Smith, Billie Holiday, Count Basie, Bob Dylan and Bruce Springsteen?

12 Which French composer is famous for his use of birdsong?

13 Which opera takes place in Catfish Row?

14 Who had a hit with *My Guy* in the Sixties?

15 Who switched on Bach and then changed sex?

1 Who composed *La Marseillaise*?

2 Where is Mozart's *Magic Flute* set?

3 Who wrote *Take Five*?

4 What is the name of Mahler's symphony no.1?

5 Which Irish composer influenced Chopin and was praised by Schumann?

6 J.S. Bach's *Musical Offering* was written on a theme by whom?

7 Who composed the symphonic poems *The Rock* and *The Isle of the Dead*?

8 Identify and link: Cosima, Hans, Marie, Richard and Franz.

9 Who were the original members of Fleetwood Mac?

10 What are the names of Tchaikovsky's first, second and sixth symphonies?

11 Which singer and which guitarist wrote *Fa-Fa-Fa-Fa-Fa*?

12 What was Muddy Waters' real name?

13 Who wrote the words to Schumann's *Dichterliebe*?

14 Who wrote and first had a hit with *Shake, Rattle and Roll*?

15 Where is the Grosses Festspielhaus?

SOUNDS QUESTIONS

1 Who is renowned for having taught the composers Lennox Berkeley, Walter Piston and Aaron Copland among others?

2 Which Italian musical term means 'joke'?

3 What name is given to a piece of music in the style of a Venetian gondolier's song?

4 What was 'Diabolus in musica'?

5 What is the 'Devil's Trill'?

6 Who composed *Take the A Train*?

7 Which is Britain's heaviest bell?

8 Which instrument did Sir Malcolm Arnold play as a member of the London Philharmonic Orchestra?

9 Who wrote the soundtrack to the Otto Preminger film *Anatomy of a Murder*?

10 Which composer ran a successful insurance business?

11 Who were the four members of the 'supergroup' Blind Faith?

12 Who are the members of the Amadeus Quartet?

13 Who wrote the English lyric to *My Way*?

14 Which composer wrote his symphony No. 4 *In Memory of Dylan Thomas*?

15 Where would you find a *dux* and a *comes*, and what are they?

1 What is a calliope?

2 Who was the 'English' Bach?

3 Who were Pres, Bags, Bean and Bird?

4 Who was the first nationally popular jazz musician to run a racially mixed band?

5 Who composed *Handel in the Strand* and *Molly on the Shore*?

6 What was Stevie Wonder's first UK top twenty hit?

7 Name four of the composers known as 'the Five', or 'the Mighty Handful'?

8 Which opera is based on the life of the astronomer Kepler?

9 Who first had hits with *I Heard it Through the Grapevine* and *Lean on Me*?

10 For what was François Tourte renowned?

11 Who sang *As Time Goes By* in the film *Casablanca*?

12 Which composer wrote film music for *King Lear* in 1970?

13 How old was Vincenzo Bellini when he died?

14 Who had a hit with the song *Puppy Love* in 1972?

15 What was Beethoven's only oratorio?

1 *Miracle, London,* and *Schoolmaster* are all symphonies by whom?

2 To which instrument does an orchestra normally tune?

3 Why do orchestral clarinettists often carry two instruments?

4 Who wrote *Blue Suede Shoes*?

5 What is the popular name for the aria *Ombra mai fù* from the opera *Xerxes*?

6 Which successful partnership began with *Don't Make Me Over*?

7 What is generally regarded as the first opera?

8 Who composed the rhapsody *An Imaginary Trip to the Faroe Islands*?

9 Which Cole Porter song was inspired by a leaky tap?

10 Which oboe is pitched between the oboe and the cor anglais?

11 Which jazz trumpeter and which concert pianist each had only one arm?

12 Who wrote the libretto of Bach's *Coffee Cantata*?

13 Who composed the tune *Body and Soul*?

14 Which composer married Constance Weber?

15 Which operas comprise Puccini's *Il Trittico*?

1 In Rome, during Holy week, a famous *Miserere* is sung. For many years its score was kept secret though Mozart wrote it down after one, or possibly two, hearings. Who wrote it?

2 What is Modest Mussorgsky's only completed opera?

3 Who composed *The Cunning Little Vixen*?

4 What is a *melisma*?

5 Name three of the composers known as 'Les Six'.

6 Who composed the tune '*Round Midnight*?

7 Who is supposed to have coined the term 'Rock 'n' Roll'?

8 Which two famous composers have 'K' numbers?

9 Who were the guitarist, bassist and drummer associated with the early success of Elvis Presley?

10 What was Bach's last, unfinished, work?

11 What are the five sections of Bach's B minor Mass?

12 Name the composers of *Faust* (the opera based on Goethe), the dramatic cantata *The Damnation of Faust* and *A Faust Symphony*.

13 Who founded the Philharmonia Orchestra and when?

14 Béla Bartók wrote the *Mikroskosmos*. What is it?

15 Who wrote the music for the films *Psycho*, *Citizen Kane* and the *Magnificent Ambersons*?

1 What are the names of Schubert's symphonies Nos. 4 and 9?

2 What nationality were Frank Martin, Arthur Honegger and Ernest Bloch?

3 Which composer wrote music for the film *Louisiana Story*?

4 Which three influential rock guitarists played with the Yardbirds?

5 Which famous composer was born in Bradford?

6 Which Czech composer produced some of his best works while deaf?

7 What is the title of Vaughan Williams's seventh symphony?

8 Who was Metastasio?

9 What was the theme tune of the Count Basie band?

10 What were the first two albums by Bob Dylan?

11 Why is Haydn's *Farewell* Symphony so named?

12 Which English composer, who died in 1453, had an international reputation?

13 What is Dizzy Gillespie's real name?

14 Name two of the three operas by Tchaikovsky based on works by Pushkin.

15 How many *Diabelli Variations* did Beethoven compose?

1 Which concert pianist became Prime Minister of his country?

2 For whom was the NBC Symphony Orchestra created?

3 Who is the Principal Conductor to the Royal Opera House?

4 Who was 'Signor Crescendo'?

5 Who were the original Supremes?

6 Who said of whom: "Too much counterpoint - and what is worse, Protestant counterpoint"?

7 What are the three Shakespeare operas by Verdi?

8 What were the first names of Glinka, Gluck and Glazunov?

9 "The best hand in England" and "The best finger of the age". Which early composer was so described?

10 Name the four members of the Monkees.

11 Who is considered to be the greatest of the Amati family of instrument makers?

12 Who composed the music to the ballet *Jazz Calendar*?

13 With which band did Ella Fitzgerald first make her name?

14 Which three singers died in a plane crash in February 1959?

15 Who wrote a symphony No. O in D minor?

1 Which is the odd one out: *La Bohème, Madame Butterfly, Tosca, La Traviata*?

2 Who wrote the melody of *Rule Britannia*?

3 Who helped found Bop, Cool and Jazz Rock?

4 To whose words did Schubert compose the song *Gretchen at the Spinning-wheel*?

5 Who was Tchaikovsky's benefactress?

6 What was the first Pink Floyd album?

7 Which instrument is called *Bratsche* in Germany?

8 Who composed *Divine Poem* and *Poem of Ecstasy*?

9 Which instruments are associated with J.J. Johnson, James P. Johnson and 'Bunk' Johnson?

10 Who composed *Sinfonia Domestica*?

11 What is a Gamelan?

12 In what field was Borodin distinguished apart from in music?

13 Link Romeo, Peter and an orange.

14 What is a 'paradiddle'?

15 For whom did Stravinsky write the *Ebony Concerto* for clarinet?

1 Who wrote *Blue Moon*?

2 In music what is the origin of the word 'scale'?

3 Who said "Folk melodies are a real model of the highest artistic perfection"?

4 Which orchestra did George Szell conduct from 1946-70?

5 Who composed the "Psalmus Hungaricus" and the opera *Háry János*?

6 Who developed the jazz technique known as 'sheets of sound'?

7 Who composed the music to the ballet *Checkmate* and to the film *Things to Come*?

8 In an Indian raga, what is an *alapa*?

9 What is the pianist Erroll Garner's best known composition?

10 Place the following composers in chronological order: Rossini, Marc-Antoine Charpentier, Mascagni and Haydn.

11 Who said 'When you find yourself in the thick of it, help yourself to a bit of what is all around you'?

12 Which composer committed suicide in 1930?

13 Works by which 19th century composer and organist did Liszt once describe as deserving a "place beside the masterpieces of Bach"?

14 What nationality was the composer Michael Praetorius?

15 Which musicians are awarded the Carl Flesch and Dimitri Mitropoulos prizes?

1 What is the relative minor key to E major?

2 Who was Mozart's gifted sister?

3 Which instrument is played with a damp finger?

4 Which member of the Couperin family was known as 'le Grand'?

5 What nationality was the composer Franz Berwald?

6 The term 'song without words' primarily refers to piano works by which composer?

7 What song contains the line: "A winter's day. In a deep and dark December"?

8 Who sang *Why do Fools Fall in Love* and *I'm Not a Juvenile Delinquent*?

9 What was Mahler's last word?

10 How did Anton Webern die?

11 On which poem is the Gilbert and Sullivan opera *Princess Ida* based?

12 What are the four most common types of saxophone?

13 How is international concert pitch expressed?

14 Which instruments comprise the Modern Jazz Quartet?

15 The film *Round Midnight* is loosely based on the lives of two musicians. Who were they?

1 Which Spanish composer drowned in the English Channel?

2 Who played the Harry Lime theme in *The Third Man*?

3 Debussy, Maeterlinck, Sibelius, Fauré. What is the connection?

4 What involved Lillian Hellman, Leonard Bernstein and Voltaire?

5 Which composer is generally credited with having been the most prolific?

6 Who wrote the opera *The Saint of Bleecker Street*?

7 How many strings has a modern double bass?

8 The *musette* was a fashionable instrument in France in the seventeenth and eighteenth centuries. What was it?

9 Who wrote *Three flabby preludes (for a dog)*?

10 What did Plato describe as the three perfect instruments?

11 Which poet inspired Debussy's *Prelude à l'après-midi d'un Faune*?

12 What was known as 'king of instruments'?

13 Which doesn't belong: *The King and I, Gigi, South Pacific, The Sound of Music*?

14 Who wrote *Watermelon Man*?

15 Who wrote *Love the One You're With*?

SOUNDS ANSWERS

1 Leonard Bernstein.
2 The trombone.
3 Joseph Haydn (originally for the Austrian national anthem).
4 Enrico Caruso with *Vesti la giubba* from Leoncavallo's *I Pagliacci*.
5 *Sgt. Pepper's Lonely Hearts Club Band. With a Little Help From my Friends. Lucy in the Sky with Diamonds.*
6 Isaac Albéniz.
7 Johann Strauss the Elder.
8 The pianist Art Tatum.
9 The writer Alessandro Manzoni.
10 Hugo von Hofmannsthal.
11 Anton Stadler.
12 No. 1 in C minor, No. 2 in D major, No. 3 in F major and No. 4 in E minor.
13 The Miracles with *Shop Around*.
14 Rimsky-Korsakov.
15 Paul Whiteman.

1 George and Ira Gershwin (*Fascinating Rhythm*), Rodgers and Hart (*My Funny Valentine*), Vincent Youmans and Irving Caesar (*Tea for Two*).
2 Polly.
3 *Come On* (by Chuck Berry), *I Wanna Be Your Man* (by Lennon and McCartney) *Not Fade Away* (by Buddy Holly).
4 Heitor Villa-Lobos.
5 Eleanor Gough McKay.
6 *This is My Song* (Theme from *A Countess from Hong Kong*) sung by Petula Clark.
7 *Spem in alium.*
8 E.M. Forster and Eric Crozier.
9 Sibelius.
10 *The Ballad of John and Yoko* in 1969.
11 Producer John Hammond.
12 Olivier Messiaen.
13 *Porgy and Bess.*
14 Mary Wells.
15 Walter Carlos who recorded *Switched-On Bach*, became Wendy Carlos.

1 C. Rouget de Lisle.
2 Egypt.
3 Paul Desmond, the saxophonist of the Dave Brubeck quartet.
4 *The Titan.*
5 John Field.
6 Frederick the Great of Prussia.
7 Rachmaninov.
8 Franz Liszt lived with the Countess Marie d'Agoult by whom he fathered Cosima who married Hans von Bülow and then Richard Wagner.
9 Peter Green, John McVie, Mick Fleetwood, Jeremy Spencer.
10 *Winter Daydreams, Little Russian* and *Pathétique.*
11 Otis Redding and Steve Cropper.
12 McKinley Morganfield.
13 Heinrich Heine.
14 Joe Turner.
15 Salzburg.

4

1 Nadia Boulanger.
2 *Scherzo.*
3 A *barcarolle.*
4 The 'Devil in Music': a discordant interval (the augmented fourth), which was banned in the Middle Ages.
5 The nickname given to a sonata by Tartini supposedly inspired by Satan.
6 Billy Strayhorn.
7 Great Paul in St Paul's Cathedral.
8 The trumpet.
9 Duke Ellington.
10 Charles Ives.
11 Eric Clapton, Steve Winwood, Ginger Baker and Rick Grech.
12 Norbert Brainin, Sigmund Nissel, Peter Schidlof, Martin Lovett.
13 Paul Anka.
14 Daniel Jones.
15 In a canon. The *dux* (leader or antecedent) is the first voice to enter with the melody. The *comes* (follower or consequent) is an imitating voice.

1 A mechanical steam organ.
2 Johann Christian Bach.
3 Jazz musicians Lester Young, Milt Jackson, Coleman Hawkins and Charlie Parker.
4 Benny Goodman.
5 Percy Grainger.
6 *Uptight (Everything's Alright)* released in 1966.
7 Borodin, Cui, Mussorgsky, Rimsky-Korsakov, Balakirev.
8 Hindemith's *Die Harmonie der Welt.*
9 Gladys Knight and the Pips, and Bill Withers.
10 The making of violin bows.
11 Dooley Wilson.
12 Dimitri Shostakovich.
13 33.
14 Donny Osmond.
15 *Christ on the Mount of Olives.*

1 Haydn.
2 Oboe.
3 They are in different keys, A and B flat, for ease of playing in different pieces of music.
4 Carl Perkins.
5 Handel's *Largo.*
6 The songwriters - Burt Bacharach and Hal David with the singer Dionne Warwick.
7 Jacopo Peri's *Dafne* (1597).
8 Carl Nielsen.
9 *Night and Day.*
10 The oboe d'amore.
11 Wingy Manone and Paul Wittgenstein.
12 Picander.
13 John Green.
14 Mozart.
15 *Il Tabarro* (*The Cloak*), *Suor Angelica* (*Sister Angelica*) and *Gianni Schicchi.*

1 Gregorio Allegri.
2 *Boris Godunov.*
3 Leŏs Janáček.
4 A number of notes sung to a single syllable.
5 L. Durey, A. Honegger, D. Milhaud, G. Tailleferre, G. Auric and F. Poulenc.
6 Thelonius Monk.
7 The DJ Alan Freed.
8 Mozart (K stands for the cataloguer Köchel) and Domenico Scarlatti (K stands for the cataloguer Kirkpatrick).
9 Scotty Moore, Bill Black and D.J. Fontana.
10 *The Art of Fugue.*
11 Kyrie, Gloria, Credo, Sanctus, Agnus Dei.
12 Gounod, Berlioz and Liszt.
13 Walter Legge in 1945.
14 A piano course consisting of 153 graded pieces.
15 Bernard Herrmann.

1 *Tragic* and *Great.*
2 Swiss. (The last mentioned, became a naturalized American).
3 Virgil Thomson.
4 Eric Clapton, Jeff Beck and Jimmy Page.
5 Frederick Delius.
6 Smetana.
7 *Sinfonia Antartica* based on his own score to the film *Scott of the Antarctic* (1948).
8 An 18th century Italian poet and librettist whose works were set to music numerous times by various composers.
9 *One O'clock Jump.*
10 *Bob Dylan* and *The Freewheelin' Bob Dylan.*
11 When originally performed the musicians left the stage as their parts finished.
12 John Dunstable.
13 John Birks Gillespie.
14 *Eugene Onegin, Mazeppa* (based on the poem *Poltava*) and *The Queen of Spades.*
15 33.

1 Ignacy Paderewski. He became Prime Minister of Poland in 1919.
2 Arturo Toscanini.
3 Jeffrey Tate.
4 Gioachino Rossini.
5 Diana Ross, Mary Wilson, Florence Ballard (and Barbara Martin who dropped out in 1962).
6 Sir Thomas Beecham on Bach.
7 *Otello, Falstaff* and *Macbeth*.
8 Mikhail Ivanovich, Christoph Willibad and Alexander Kostantinovich.
9 Orlando Gibbons (composer, organist and virginalist 1583-1625).
10 Mike Nesmith, Peter Tork, Mickey Dolenz and Davy Jones.
11 Nicola Amati, the teacher of both Antonio Stradivari and Andrea Guarneri.
12 Richard Rodney Bennett.
13 The Chick Webb Band.
14 Buddy Holly, Big Bopper and Ritchie Valens.
15 Anton Bruckner.

1 *La Traviata* - by Verdi. The others are Puccini operas.
2 Thomas Augustine Arne.
3 The trumpeter Miles Davies.
4 Goethe's.
5 Nadezhda von Meck.
6 *The Piper at the Gates of Dawn* in 1967.
7 The viola.
8 Skryabin.
9 Trombone, piano and trumpet.
10 Richard Strauss.
11 A percussive orchestra of Indonesia, of influence on composers such as Debussy (or an instrument similar to the xylophone found in such an orchestra).
12 He was a professor of chemistry.
13 Prokofiev's *Romeo and Juliet, Peter and the Wolf* and *The Love for Three Oranges*.
14 A rudiment of drumming.
15 Woody Herman.

1 Rodgers and Hart.
2 From the Italian *scala* - a ladder or staircase.
3 Béla Bartók.
4 The Cleveland Orchestra.
5 Zoltán Kodály.
6 The saxophonist John Coltrane.
7 Sir Arthur Bliss.
8 The non-rhythmic introduction that sets the mood.
9 *Misty*.
10 Marc-Antoine Charpentier c1645-1704, Haydn 1732-1809,Rossini 1792-1868, and Mascagni 1863-1945.
11 Paul McCartney - in the song *Martha My Dear*.
12 Peter Warlock.
13 César Franck.
14 German.
15 Violinists and conductors.

1 C sharp minor.
2 Maria Anna ('Nannerl') Mozart.
3 The glass harmonica. The rims are stroked to produce sound.
4 François Couperin.
5 Swedish.
6 Mendelssohn.
7 *I Am a Rock* by Simon and Garfunkel.
8 Frankie Lymon and the Teenagers.
9 Mozart.
10 He was accidentally shot by an American soldier.
11 Tennyson's *The Princess*.
12 Soprano, alto, tenor, baritone.
13 The note A above middle C has 440 vibrations per second.
14 Piano, vibraphone, bass and drums.
15 Bud Powell and Lester Young.

1 Enrique Granados in 1916. His passenger ship was torpedoed by a German submarine.
2 Anton Karas.
3 Maeterlinck's drama *Pelléas et Mélisande*. It was the subject of Debussy's opera and both Sibelius and Fauré wrote incidental music for it.
4 *Candide*. Lillian Hellman wrote the book to the original musical and Leonard Bernstein composed the music. The story was based on Voltaire's *Candide*.
5 Georg Philipp Telemann.
6 Gian Carlo Menotti.
7 Either four or five.
8 A small bagpipe.
9 Erik Satie.
10 The flute, lyre and human voice.
11 Stéphane Mallarmé.
12 The organ.
13 *Gigi*, the only one to be scored by Lerner and Loewe. Rodgers and Hammerstein wrote the music for the other three.
14 Herbie Hancock.
15 Stephen Stills.

IMAGES QUESTIONS

1 Place in order of birth: Leonardo, Masaccio, Raphael, Michelangelo.

2 Who illustrated *Les Très Riches Heures* for the Duc de Berry?

3 Who co-wrote the script for *Citizen Kane* with Orson Welles?

4 Who designed the Menai suspension Bridge?

5 Which singer starred in the film *The Emperor Jones*?

6 Which film first made Rudolph Valentino a star?

7 Who illustrated both Oscar Wilde's *Salomé* and Alexander Pope's *Rape of the Lock*?

8 Which Austro-British painter was awarded the CBE in 1959?

9 In which city is the Alte Pinakothek gallery?

10 Who designed the Statue of Liberty?

11 What are 'voussoirs'?

12 Which Theodore Dreiser novel was filmed as *A Place in the Sun*?

13 Who are said to have "built like Titans and finished like goldsmiths"?

14 Where were Velázquez and Murillo born?

15 Which painter appears prominently in Boswell's *Life of Johnson*?

IMAGES QUESTIONS

1 In painting, what is an odalisque?

2 Which British Prime Minister had a son who was a well known film director?

3 Which artist is noted for a gold salt-cellar, a vivid autobiography and a bronze statue of Perseus?

4 Who painted the 'Madonna with the Long Neck'?

5 What is 'impasto'?

6 Which Polanski film is set on a Northumbrian island?

7 Who starred opposite Judy Garland in *A Star is Born*?

8 Which painter, who lived from 1878-1961 had a sister who was also a painter?

9 Which press did William Morris set up in 1891?

10 Who directed the film *Kes*?

11 What was Titian's surname?

12 What is a serif?

13 What term is used to describe the network of fine cracks on the surface of an old painting?

14 Which movement is associated with Vladimir Tatlin, Naum Gabo and Antoine Pevsner?

15 What were the first names of the three painters named Bellini?

IMAGES QUESTIONS 3

1   Who is the connection between the films *High Noon, The Nun's Story,* and *A Man For All Seasons?*

2   What is 'boiserie'?

3   Which novel is the film *Apocalypse Now* loosely based upon?

4   Who was the first actor to be knighted?

5   Who directed the film *The Shop around the Corner* and who were its two main stars?

6   Which London society of painters was founded in 1911 under the inspiration of Walter Sickert?

7   Which arts movement developed at the Cabaret Voltaire?

8   Which form of modern art is particularly associated with Victor Vasarély?

9   Who designed the gardens of Versailles?

10   Who did the caricature *The Plum Pudding in Danger?*

11   Who won an Oscar as best supporting actor for the film *Ryan's Daughter?*

12   Which father and son won Oscars for the film *The Treasure of the Sierra Madre?*

13   In which film did Henry Fonda win the gunfight at the O.K. corral?

14   Which Michelangelo painting was 'censored' by Daniele da Volterra?

15   What was Ronald Reagan's last feature film?

IMAGES QUESTIONS 4

1 In which film does Jean Gabin escape from Erich von Stroheim?

2 Who designed the Marble Arch?

3 In architecture, what are 'volutes'?

4 Who originally illustrated *Oliver Twist*?

5 Who was the first English painter to receive a peerage?

6 Who painted 'The Naked Maja' and who was she?

7 Who directed *Shoeshine*?

8 What is 'frottage'?

9 What is a 'pietà'?

10 In art what is the definition of the Golden Mean?

11 Which composers are the subjects of the films *Song of Love, A Song to Remember* and *Song Without End*?

12 Which painter worked as a diplomat and was knighted by Charles I?

13 Which film features the characters Eddie Mars and Carmen Sternwood?

14 In which 1951, 1952 and 1954 films did Elia Kazan direct Marlon Brando?

15 What is 'cloisonné'?

1   Who directed *Wild Strawberries*?

2   Who said: "Mother of mercy, is this the end of Rico"?

3   What is *cire perdue*?

4   What are the three basic parts of a classical column?

5   Who designed the Seagram Building in New York?

6   What nationality was the sculptor Brancusi?

7   In which film did Fred Astaire sing *Night and Day*?

8   Where was the painter James Ensor born?

9   In John Huston's film *The Maltese Falcon,* who played Sam Spade, Brigid O'Shaughnessy, Kasper Gutman and Joel Cairo?

10   Who painted 'Whaam'?

11   Who commissioned Michelangelo to paint the ceiling of the Sistine Chapel?

12   Name all five Marx Brothers and two of their real names.

13   Who directed *Closely Observed Trains*?

14   Which sculptor set up 'The Store' in which he sold plaster replicas of food?

15   Which singer is portrayed in *Coal Miner's Daughter*?

1 Who directed *The Sound of Music*?

2 Who designed the dome of Florence Cathedral?

3 What term denotes the prevailing tendency in Italian art from c1520-1600?

4 Who directed *Casablanca*?

5 What name is given to a painting or carving on three adjacent panels?

6 For which film did Jane Fonda first win an Oscar?

7 What is Jan van Eyck's most celebrated work and who else may have been involved?

8 What were the first three full length feature films directed by John Schlesinger?

9 Which American painter went bankrupt suing John Ruskin?

10 Who directed *Berlin Olympiad* and who directed *Tokyo Olympiad*?

11 In which film was the pellet with the poison in the chalice from the palace - or not!?

12 In Christian art, what is a 'glory'?

13 Which three organizations collectively became "The Royal Ballet" in 1956?

14 Which artist originated the 'mobile'?

15 Who was a founder and first artistic director of the New York City Ballet?

1 In which film does Alec Guinness play eight roles?

2 Who were the architects of the Pompidou Centre?

3 Place in chronological order: Rococo, Neo-classical, Gothic and Romanesque?

4 Who designed the famous library at Trinity College Cambridge?

5 Of what type of painting was Richard Cosway a noted exponent?

6 Who was the first black performer to win an acting Oscar?

7 In which film are Dashiell Hammett and Lillian Hellman lovers?

8 Which classic gangster film is subtitled 'The Shame of a Nation'?

9 Which ballet company achieved world status under the leadership of John Cranko?

10 Who was director of photography for *Close Encounters of the Third Kind*?

11 What is 'Cosmati' work?

12 Who were the two architects of the Houses of Parliament?

13 Which ballet was originally entitled *Chopiniana*?

14 Which Manet paintings shocked Paris in 1863 and 1865?

15 Where is Michelangelo's 'Moses'?

1 Which was the first film in which Greta Garbo spoke?

2 Who sculpted 'Balzac', 'Victor Hugo' and 'The Burghers of Calais'?

3 Which painting gave rise to the term 'impressionism'?

4 In which film does Gene Kelly dance with a cartoon mouse?

5 How did Gerald Crich die in *Women in Love*?

6 What are the three films of Wajda's trilogy about the experiences of wartime Poland?

7 Who painted the landmark work 'Oath of the Horatii'?

8 Who designed the Paris Opéra?

9 What was Cary Grant's original name?

10 Which actress is the subject of Reynold's painting 'Tragic Muse'?

11 Which film star said, while reading the Bible on his death bed: "I'm looking for loopholes"?

12 Which 16th century German artist used signatures of a winged dragon, and the initials LC?

13 The seminal painter Tommaso di Giovanni di Simone Guidi is better known by his nickname. What is it?

14 What is *sotto in sù*?

15 Where did the seven 'road' films lead for Bob Hope, Bing Crosby and Dorothy Lamour?

1   What are the primary colours of pigment?

2   Which two actors portrayed Raffles in films in 1930 and 1939?

3   Who wrote the music to Eisentein's film *Alexander Nevsky*?

4   Who choreographed *West Side Story*?

5   Who designed the Guggenheim Museum?

6   Who played Richard Hannay in the 1935, 1959 and 1978 versions of *The Thirty Nine Steps*?

7   In which film does Alfred Hitchcock appear carrying a double bass?

8   Name two feature films for which John Ford won Oscars.

9   What is 'egg-and-dart'?

10   Name the films of Satyajit Ray's *Apu Trilogy*.

11   Who trained Leonardo da Vinci?

12   Who formed the Dance Theatre of Harlem?

13   Who painted 'The Rokeby Venus'?

14   Who designed the Royal Courts of Justice in the Strand?

15   Which was the first Mickey Mouse cartoon?

1   What did the title of Fellini's *8½* refer to?

2   What was the Bauhaus, who founded it, and where?

3   For which film did Humphrey Bogart win an Oscar?

4   What is *sfumato*?

5   Who created the Muppets?

6   Who said: "I can control the flow of paint"?

7   What were *Les Fauves* (the wild beasts) and who led them?

8   Which composer exhibited wth the Blue Rider group of artists?

9   What is the name for an ornamental screen at the back of an altar in a church?

10   What was the first feature film directed by Roman Polanski?

11   Why was the sculptor Pietro Torrigiano exiled from Florence?

12   In 1905 which choreographer created 'The Dying Swan' solo and for which ballerina?

13   Which influential photographer was killed in Vietnam in 1954?

14   In which city is much of *The Battleship Potemkin* set?

15   Who coined the term 'art brut'?

1   In which films did Groucho Marx play the characters Otis B. Driftwood and Dr. Hugo Z. Hackenbush?

2   Who designed the Church of the Sagrada Familia in Barcelona?

3   Who directed the film *Andrei Rublev*?

4   Of which young Cornishman did Reynolds remark ".... like Caravaggio, but finer!"?

5   Which British architects planned New Delhi?

6   Where is the 'Laughing Cavalier'?

7   Who has been called 'the English Palladio'?

8   What are the five classical orders of architecture?

9   Who played the singer/pianist in *To Have and Have Not*?

10   Who first choreographed Stravinsky's *The Rite of Spring*?

11   Who illustrated the books *Rip Van Winkle* and *Peter Pan*?

12   Which great painter abducted a nun?

13   In which film is Sherlock Holmes treated by Sigmund Freud?

14   How was the cubist painter José Victoriano Gonzalez better known?

15   Who directed *Five Easy Pieces*?

1 What nationality was the painter Edvard Munch?

2 Who carved the choir stalls in St Paul's Cathedral?

3 Who played the title roles in *The Good, The Bad and The Ugly*?

4 Who succeeded Sir Frederick Ashton as director of the Royal Ballet in 1970?

5 What are the titles of Kurosawa's versions of *Macbeth* and *King Lear*?

6 Which artist did Martin Luther describe as "one who was the best of men"?

7 For which two films has Elizabeth Taylor won Oscars?

8 Which artist painted Oliver Cromwell "warts, and everything"?

9 Of which film was *High Society* a musical reworking?

10 Name the Hitler and Mussolini characters in Chaplin's film *The Great Dictator*.

11 In which film does François Truffaut play a UFO researcher?

12 What is a 'caryatid'?

13 Which artist gave up painting to concentrate on chess?

14 Who was the first child actor to earn a million dollars?

15 Which architect is noted for his designs of London tube stations, of which Southgate station is an outstanding example?

1   Which woman said in which classic film: "I *am* big. It's the pictures that got small"?

2   For what is the 16th century painter and architect Giorgio Vasari best known?

3   Who painted 'The Leaping Horse' and 'Salisbury Cathedral From the Bishop's Grounds'?

4   What is *contrapposto*?

5   Which Ray Bradbury novel was filmed by François Truffaut?

6   Who designed the British Museum?

7   Which musical is based on Damon Runyon's *The Idyll of Miss Sarah Brown*?

8   What was the first successful British feature film with sound dialogue?

9   What is an 'ogee' arch?

10   In ballet, what is an attitude?

11   Which Swiss painter described his work as "taking a line for a walk"?

12   In which ballet does Aurora dance the title role?

13   For which films did Sir Cecil Beaton win Oscars?

14   Which ballet, first performed in 1917, had music by Satie, choreography by Massine, a libretto by Cocteau and scenery and costumes by Picasso?

15   On which two films did Salvador Dali and Luís Buñuel collaborate?

IMAGES ANSWERS

1 Masaccio (1401), Leonardo (1452), Michelangelo (1475), Raphael (1483).
2 The Limbourg brothers - Herman, Jean and Pol.
3 Herman J. Mankiewicz.
4 Thomas Telford.
5 Paul Robeson.
6 *The Four Horsemen of the Apocalypse* (1921).
7 Aubrey Beardsley.
8 Oskar Kokoschka.
9 Munich.
10 Frédéric Auguste Bartholdi.
11 The wedge-shaped stones which form an arch.
12 *An American Tragedy.*
13 The Mogul emperors.
14 Seville.
15 Joshua Reynolds.

1 A voluptuous female figure in a quasi Turkish setting.
2 H.H. Asquith - father of Anthony Asquith.
3 Benvenuto Cellini.
4 Parmigianino.
5 The thick application of oil or similar paint to a canvas, or the thickness and texture of such paint when applied.
6 *Cul de Sac.*
7 James Mason.
8 Augustus John - his sister was Gwen John.
9 The Kelmscott Press.
10 Ken Loach.
11 Vecelli (or Vecellio).
12 A short line finishing off the stroke of a letter, especially at the top or bottom of a printed capital.
13 *Craquelure.*
14 Constructivism.
15 Jacopo, and his sons Gentile and Giovanni.

1 They were directed by Fred Zinnemann.
2 Carved wood panelling.
3 Conrad's *Heart of Darkness*.
4 Sir Henry Irving.
5 Ernst Lubitsch. James Stewart and Margaret Sullavan co-starred.
6 The Camden Town Group.
7 Dadaism.
8 Op art.
9 André le Nôtre.
10 James Gillray.
11 Sir John Mills, who played an idiot.
12 Walter Huston for Best Supporting Actor and his son John for Best Director.
13 *My Darling Clementine* (1946).
14 The Last Judgement. He painted draperies to cover the nudity of some of the figures.
15 *The Killers* (1964). He played a corrupt businessman.

1 *La Grande Illusion* (1937).
2 John Nash.
3 Spiral or scroll-shaped ornaments.
4 George Cruikshank.
5 Lord Leighton.
6 Goya, the Duchess of Alba, with whom the painter is thought to have had an affair.
7 Vittorio De Sica.
8 A technique for producing surface designs in which paper is placed on an uneven surface and rubbed with crayon or pencil.
9 A representation of the Virgin Mary lamenting over the dead Christ.
10 A straight line divided so that the lesser part is to the greater as the greater is to the whole (approx. 8:13).
11 Schumann, Chopin and Liszt.
12 Sir Peter Paul Rubens.
13 *The Big Sleep*.
14 *A Streetcar Named Desire*, *Viva Zapata* and *On the Waterfront*.
15 Multicoloured decorative work in which enamels are applied between metal strips or wire borders fixed to a surface.

1 Ingmar Bergman.
2 Edward G. Robinson at the end of *Little Caesar*.
3 The 'lost wax' process - an ancient technique for casting a sculpture in metal - usually bronze.
4 A base, a shaft and a capital.
5 Mies van der Rohe and Philip Johnson.
6 Romanian.
7 *The Gay Divorcee* (1934).
8 Belgium.
9 Humphrey Bogart, Mary Astor, Sydney Greenstreet and Peter Lorre.
10 Roy Lichtenstein.
11 Pope Julius II.
12 Groucho (Julius), Harpo ([Adolph] Arthur), Chico (Leonard), Zeppo (Herbert), and Gummo (Milton).
13 Jiri Menzel.
14 Claes Oldenburg.
15 Loretta Lynn.

1 Robert Wise.
2 Filippo Brunelleschi.
3 Mannerism.
4 Michael Curtiz.
5 A triptych.
6 *Klute* (1971).
7 'The Adoration of the Lamb' - the great altarpiece in the cathedral at Ghent. It bears an inscription - probably unreliable - that credits Jan's brother Hubert as its principal creator.
8 *A Kind of Loving* (1962), *Billy Liar* (1963) and *Darling* (1965).
9 James MacNeill Whistler.
10 Leni Riefenstahl and Kon Ichikawa.
11 *The Court Jester*.
12 A depiction - like a halo - of radiance around a holy figure.
13 Sadler's Wells Ballet, Sadler's Wells Theatre Ballet, and Sadler's Wells School.
14 Alexander Calder.
15 George Balanchine.

1 *Kind Hearts and Coronets* (1948).
2 Richard Rogers and Renzo Piano.
3 Romanesque, Gothic, Rococo, Neo-classical.
4 Sir Christopher Wren.
5 Portrait miniatures.
6 Hattie McDaniel as Best Supporting Actress for *Gone with the Wind* (1939).
7 *Julia.*
8 *Scarface.*
9 The Stuttgart Ballet.
10 Vilmos Zsigmond.
11 A type of highly decorative mosaic.
12 Sir Charles Barry and A.W.N. Pugin.
13 *Les Sylphides.*
14 'Dejeuner sur l'herbe' and 'Olympia'.
15 At the Church of S. Pietro in Vincoli, Rome.

1 *Anna Christie.*
2 Rodin.
3 Monet's 'Impression, Sunrise' (1871).
4 *Anchors Aweigh* (1945).
5 He froze to death.
6 *A Generation, Kanal* and *Ashes and Diamonds.*
7 Jacques-Louis David.
8 Charles Garnier.
9 Archibald Leach.
10 Sarah Siddons.
11 W.C. Fields.
12 Lucas Cranach.
13 Masaccio (Big or hulking Thomas).
14 It is Italian for 'From below upwards' and applies to a method of foreshortening in ceiling decoration composition whereby figures are made to appear floating or suspended in space.
15 Singapore, Zanzibar, Morocco, Utopia, Rio, Bali and Hong Kong.

1 Red, yellow and blue.
2 Ronald Colman and David Niven.
3 Prokofiev.
4 Jerome Robbins.
5 Frank Lloyd Wright.
6 Robert Donat, Kenneth More and Robert Powell.
7 *Strangers on a Train.*
8 *The Informer, The Grapes of Wrath, How Green Was My Valley* and *The Quiet Man.*
9 A type of architectural moulding consisting of eggs alternating with arrow-heads.
10 *Pather Panchali, The Unvanquished, The World of Apu.*
11 Verrocchio.
12 Arthur Mitchell.
13 Velázquez.
14 George Edmund Street.
15 *Plane Crazy* (1928).

1 The number of films he had made.
2 A progressive art and design school founded by Walter Gropius in Weimar in 1919.
3 *The African Queen* (1951).
4 The gradual and almost imperceptible transition between colours or tones.
5 Jim Henson.
6 Jackson Pollock.
7 A group of artists in France in the early 20th century led by Matisse.
8 Arnold Schoenberg.
9 A reredos.
10 *Knife In the Water* (1962).
11 For breaking Michelangelo's nose.
12 Michel Fokine for Anna Pavlova.
13 Robert Capa.
14 Odessa.
15 Jean Dubuffet.

1 *A Night at the Opera* and *A Day at the Races*.
2 Antonio Gaudi.
3 Andrei Tarkovsky.
4 John Opie, the 'Cornish Wonder'.
5 Sir Edwin Lutyens and Sir Herbert Baker.
6 In London's Wallace Collection.
7 Inigo Jones.
8 Doric, Ionic, Corinthian, Tuscan and Composite.
9 Hoagy Carmichael.
10 Nijinsky.
11 Arthur Rackham.
12 Fra Filippo Lippi.
13 *The Seven Per Cent Solution*.
14 Juan Gris.
15 Bob Rafelson.

1 Norwegian.
2 Grinling Gibbons.
3 Clint Eastwood, Lee Van Cleef, Eli Wallach.
4 Kenneth MacMillan (at first with John Field).
5 *Throne of Blood* and *Ran*.
6 Albrecht Dürer.
7 *Butterfield 8* (1960) and *Who's Afraid of Virginia Woolf* (1966).
8 Sir Peter Lely.
9 *The Philadelphia Story* (1940).
10 Adenoid Hynkel and Benzino Napaloni.
11 "Close Encounters of the Third Kind".
12 A pillar or support carved in the shape of a draped female figure.
13 Marcel Duchamp.
14 Jackie Coogan.
15 Charles Holden.

1 Gloria Swanson in *Sunset Boulevard* (1950).
2 As a biographer of Renaissance artists.
3 John Constable.
4 A posture in sculpture or painting in which one section of the body (such as the top half) is twisted in opposition to the other.
5 *Fahrenheit 451*.
6 Sir Robert Smirke.
7 *Guys and Dolls*.
8 Hitchcock's *Blackmail* (1929).
9 An arch curving outwards and then inwards to form a point at the top.
10 A pose in which one leg is raised and bent either behind or in front of the dancer.
11 Paul Klee.
12 *Sleeping Beauty*.
13 *Gigi* and *My Fair Lady*.
14 *Parade*.
15 *Un Chien Andalou* (1928) and *L'Age D'Or* (1930).

1 Who was chief of the German General Staff at the outbreak of World War I?

2 What were the former professions of Margaret Thatcher?

3 Who was the first man to reach the North Pole?

4 Which famous detective writer was jailed for 'un-American activities'?

5 Which English painter killed his father?

6 Which influential 19th century mathematician died aged 20?

7 What does the name Molotov signify in Russian?

8 Who said in 1910 'You see in me the last monarch of the old school'?

9 Who discovered the tomb of Tutankhamen?

10 What do the following Popes have in common: Leo X, Clement VII, Pius IV?

11 Who was Nelson's wife?

12 Who were the two husbands of Eleanor of Aquitaine?

13 What was Neil Kinnock's university degree in?

14 Which statesman wrote *The Edge of the Sword* and *The Army of the Future*?

15 What was Winston Churchill's mother's maiden name?

1 Who was the first woman to fly solo across the Atlantic?

2 Who is the President of the Royal Society?

3 Which poets worked as secretaries for Oliver Cromwell?

4 From whom did the infant Dr Johnson receive the royal touch for scrofula?

5 Who was the first person known to have sailed solo around the world?

6 Which saint taught Thomas Aquinas and was known as 'The Universal Doctor'?

7 Who said "when I was a boy, the Sioux owned the world"?

8 Which poet married Isadora Duncan?

9 Which two brothers wrote *The Two Magics* and *The Varieties of Religious Experience*?

10 Which of the following lived longest: John Keats, Charlie Parker, Jimi Hendrix, Mozart, Masaccio?

11 What was Jerome K. Jerome's middle name?

12 Who was the European discoverer of the Mississipi River?

13 Who have been the five Secretary Generals of the United Nations? ✓

14 Who received the title 'father of modern linguistics' after the posthumous publication of a series of his lecture notes?

15 Whom did Horace Walpole call 'Queen of the Methodists'?

PEOPLE QUESTIONS

1 Which king did Gaddafi depose?

2 Who were Park, Clapperton and Stanley?

3 For whom was the Taj Mahal built?

4 Who is the director of the British Museum?

5 For whom is Big Ben named?

6 What is the family name of the Marquess of Bath?

7 Who became Poet Laureate in 1843?

8 What became of the philosopher Empedocles?

9 Who was the last Hapsburg King of Spain?

10 How did Pliny the Elder die?

11 Which composer, writer and painter did the writer and critic Théophile Gautier refer to as the 'Trinity of Romantic Art'?

12 Who is credited with naming America?

13 Which rock star is buried in the same cemetery as Chopin?

14 Whom did William Pitt describe as 'A heaven-born general'?

15 Who are traditionally regarded as the first three British Prime Ministers?

PEOPLE QUESTIONS

1 Who was the Portuguese discoverer of Brazil?

2 Who was Charlemagne's father?

3 What was the Latin name of the philosopher Descartes?

4 Who was Ebenezer Howard?

5 How many books in the authorized version of the Bible are named after women?

6 In which city was Karl Marx born?

7 Who were Chang and Eng?

8 What relation was Queen Victoria to George I?

9 Which great novelist was a minister under De Gaulle?

10 Who said: "I have climbed to the top of the greasy pole"?

11 Which artists did Barbara Hepworth marry?

12 For what is the Fugger family renowned?

13 Who was chiefly responsible for creating the Trans-Siberian Railway and later became Russia's first constitutional Prime Minister?

14 Who was the first husband of Mary Queen of Scots?

15 Who is Baron Greenwich?

PEOPLE QUESTIONS

5

1 In which town are Liszt and Wagner buried?

2 Which famous psychoanalyst died in an American jail?

3 Who won both the Nobel prize for literature and an Oscar?

4 Which French statesman was nicknamed 'the Tiger'?

5 Who was the first English king to have held the title 'Prince of Wales'?

6 Which pharaoh ruled longest?

7 Who was Elizabeth Garrett Anderson's famous sister?

8 Who founded the Sikh religion?

9 How did Federico Garcia Lorca die?

10 Who were the joint authors of the comic novels *The Twelve Chairs* and *The Little Golden Calf*?

11 Which famous astronomer was a professional organist?

12 Who sat Damocles beneath a sword?

13 Supply the first names of: Rossetti (1783-1854), Rossetti (1830-94), Rossetti (1828-82), Rossetti (1829-1919)?

14 What did Stalin study at college? ✓

15 Who was the first sovereign to live in Buckingham Palace?

1 Who was Jean-Baptiste Poquelin?

2 What was Buddha's original name?

3 For what is the name Bernoulli famous?

4 In which field did the Jussieu family excel?

5 Which constituency did Churchill represent from 1945-1964?

6 Who was Helen Keller's teacher?

7 What nationality is the poet Octavio Paz?

8 Who was the European discoverer of Lake Victoria?

9 Who succeeded Martin Luther King as president of the Southern Christian Leadership Conference?

10 Which statesman was killed by a train at the opening of the Liverpool and Manchester Railway?

11 Who was the first president of Czechoslavakia?

12 Which leaders signed the Israel-Egypt peace treaty in 1979?

13 Name two of the four emperors who ruled Rome in AD 69?

14 How did Dame Nellie Melba get her name?

15 Nero murdered his mother. What was her name?

1 Who invented pêche melba?

2 Who was the principal leader of the Russian Mensheviks?

3 What were Duke Ellington's christian names?

4 Who invented Esperanto?

5 Who is known as the 'Father of the Hydrogen Bomb'?

6 Who was the first woman to be launched into space?

7 Who were the three wives of Julius Caesar?

8 What were the pseudonyms of the Brontë sisters?

9 Which poet was appointed Dean of St Paul's in 1621?

10 Who was the youngest US President?

11 Supply either the maiden or married name of George Eliot.

12 Which dramatist/architect died in 1726?

13 Which French and German statesmen shared the 1926 Nobel Peace Prize?

14 What are the family names of the dukes of Bedford, Devonshire, Norfolk and Westminster?

15 How did the Norwegian king Magnus 'Bareleg' earn his nickname?

1 What was Lord Haw Haw's real name?

2 Who assassinated Archduke Francis Ferdinand in 1914?

3 Which British sovereigns since William the Conqueror were not crowned?

4 Which British and which Brazilian statesmen committed suicide in 1822 and 1954 respectively?

5 Of which tribe was Boadicea queen?

6 Name three of the ministers of Charles II who were known collectively from their initials as the CABAL?

7 How was Henry the Navigator related to the Plantagenets?

8 Who was Prime Minister of Britain in the year of Waterloo?

9 Which Russian spy was exchanged for Greville Wynne?

10 Who was the first Bourbon king of France?

11 Who won an Oscar as best actor for the film *It Happened One Night*?

12 Name three of the seven members of the Pre-Raphaelite Brotherhood?

13 Of which study is Baron Jöns Jakob Berzelius considered to be one of the founders?

14 What is the connection between W.Somerset Maugham, Sir Arthur Conan Doyle and Che Guevara?

15 Who was the last Ottoman emperor?

1 What was Tony Benn's title before he gave it up?

2 Who was German Chancellor at the outbreak of World War I?

3 Who created Joey the Clown?

4 Who were the first three Prime Ministers of India?

5 Who was President of France at the outbreak of World War I?

6 Who was the first Romanov Tsar?

7 Which explorer established the first French claim in Canada?

8 Which Irish nationalist was elected Britain's first female MP?

9 Which Ostrogoth was king of Italy from AD 493-526?

10 An English composer had the same three names as a great poet - but in a different order. Who?

11 Which parties did Sir Oswald Mosley represent in Parliament?

12 What was the Duke of Wellington's original name?

13 Name the four US Presidents who were assassinated - in chronological order?

14 Which Elizabethan courtier was married to Amy Robsart?

15 With whom do you associate Belle Elmore and Ethel Le Neve?

1 Whom did Cicero call the 'Father of History'?

2 Who was assassinated in a Harlem ballroom in February 1965?

3 Who was the widow of Tuthmosis II, who became pharaoh?

4 What were the real names of Stalin, Lenin and Trotsky?

5 Who was the father of the Black Prince?

6 Who was first secretary of the Communist Party in Russia between the death of Stalin and the appointment of Khrushchev?

7 Who was the Prime Minister of the GDR in 1987?

8 Who was the illegitimate son of James II of England who became a a military hero in France?

9 Who founded the Red Cross and what inspired him to do so?

10 How did Louis XIV, the Sun King, earn his nickname?

11 Which composer of madrigals had his wife and her lover murdered?

12 Who is the patron saint of Paris and why?

13 Who was the first Astronomer Royal?

14 Who was Artemisia Gentileschi and when did she live?

15 Which scientist was a tax collector and died on the guillotine?

1 Who was the last Roman emperor of the west?

2 What was Charles Dickens' first job?

3 Who was "mad, bad, and dangerous to know"?

4 Which three men sat in the British cabinet in both world wars?

5 Who is the president of SWAPO?

6 Which famous writer lived in Abbotsford House?

7 Which philosopher worked as a lens grinder?

8 Who is the sovereign of Denmark?

9 Which philospher was canonized in 1323?

10 Who was the first Governor General of India?

11 Which 20th century British Prime Minister held the offices of Chancellor of the Exchequer, Home Secretary and Foreign Secretary?

12 Which Roman emperor died at York?

13 Who is regarded as the founder of modern set theory?

14 Which European religious reformer died at the Battle of Kappel in 1531?

15 Which writer had a pen name meaning 'bitter'?

1 What was Emperor Haile Selassie's original name?

2 Who was the 'Flanders Mare'?

3 On whom did Lewis Caroll base Alice?

4 Whom did Diaghilev call "My little English girl"?

5 Who were Atropos, Clotho and Lachesis?

6 In 1919 which film stars founded United Artists?

7 What was the code name of the notorious World War II spy who worked for the British ambassador in Turkey?

8 Which Tsar murdered his son in a fit of rage?

9 Who was the last British Prime Minister to lead a government as a member of the House of Lords?

10 Where was Archimedes born, where did he spend most of his life and where did he die?

11 Who was Saxo Grammaticus?

12 Who first sailed through the Northwest Passage?

13 Who was Cunobelinus?

14 Who was the first president of the Royal Academy?

15 Who founded the Universal Negro Improvement Association?

PEOPLE QUESTIONS

1 Who founded Fianna Fáil and what does it mean?

2 Who founded the dynasty of white rajas in Sarawak?

3 Who has been called 'the wisest American'?

4 Whom did Queen Anne marry?

5 Name one of the two Borgia Popes?

6 What is J.B. Lamarck famous for?

7 Who wrote the libretti for *The Marriage of Figaro, Don Giovanni* and *Cosi fan tutte*.

8 What was the real name of the writer O. Henry?

9 Which painter/novelist founded Vorticism?

10 Which 20th century architect is closely associated with the geodesic dome?

11 Who led the 'Expedition of the Thousand' - in 1860?

12 Who assassinated Mahatma Gandhi?

13 In which city is J.S. Bach buried?

14 Which great Roman poet was banished to the Black Sea?

15 Who wrote the tragedies *The Bacchae* and *Iphigenia in Aulis*?

PEOPLE ANSWERS

1 Helmuth J.L. von Moltke.
2 Research chemist and barrister.
3 Robert Peary in 1909.
4 Dashiell Hammett.
5 Richard Dadd.
6 Evariste Galois - as the result of a duel.
7 'The Hammerer'.
8 Emperor Franz-Josef of Austria-Hungary.
9 Howard Carter in 1922.
10 They were all Medici.
11 Frances Nisbet.
12 Louis VII of France and Henry II of England.
13 Industrial relations and history.
14 Charles de Gaulle.
15 Jennie Jerome.

1 Amelia Earhart.
2 Sir George Porter.
3 John Milton and Andrew Marvell.
4 Queen Anne, in 1712.
5 The Canadian Joshua Slocum in 1895-8.
6 St. Albertus Magnus.
7 Sitting Bull c 1834-93.
8 Sergey Yesenin.
9 Henry and William James - respectively.
10 Mozart - he died aged 35, Parker died at 34, Hendrix at 27, Masaccio at 26 and Keats at 25.
11 Klapka.
12 Hernando de Soto, in 1541.
13 Trygve - Lie (Norway), Dag Hammarskjöld (Sweden), U Thant (Burma), Kurt Waldheim (Austria) and Javier Perez de Cuellar (Peru).
14 Ferdinand de Saussure.
15 Selina, Countess of Huntingdon.

1 King Idris in 1969.
2 The explorers Mungo Park, Hugh Clapperton and Henry Morton Stanley.
3 Mumtaz Mahal - wife of the Mogul emperor Shah Jahan.
4 Sir David Wilson.
5 Sir Benjamin Hall - commissioner of works at the time of installation in 1859.
6 Thynne.
7 William Wordsworth.
8 He is traditionally said to have thrown himself into the crater of Mount Etna.
9 Charles II from 1665-1700.
10 He was asphyxiated during the eruption of Vesuvius in AD 79.
11 Hector Berlioz, Victor Hugo and Eugene Delacroix.
12 The map-maker Martin Waldseemüller, after Amerigo Vespucci and apparently in ignorance of the voyages of Columbus.
13 Jim Morrison of the Doors - in the Père-Lachaise cemetary in Paris.
14 Clive of India.
15 Robert Walpole, The Earl of Wilmington and Henry Pelham.

1 Pedro Alvares Cabral, in 1500.
2 Pepin the short.
3 Renatius Cartesius.
4 A town planner who founded the English garden-city.
5 Two, Ruth and Esther.
6 Trier, in the Rhineland.
7 The original Siamese twins.
8 Great great great granddaughter.
9 André Malraux, - as minister for cultural affairs for ten years.
10 Disraeli on becoming Prime Minister in 1868.
11 The sculptor John Skeaping and the painter Ben Nicholson.
12 They were a German banking family who supported Maximilian I and other Habsburg emperors.
13 Sergei Witte, 1849-1915.
14 Francis II of France.
15 It is one of the titles of the Duke of Edinburgh.

PEOPLE **ANSWERS**

1 Bayreuth.
2 Wilhelm Reich.
3 George Bernard Shaw.
4 Georges Clemenceau.
5 Edward II.
6 Phiops II (Neferkare) c94 years.
7 The feminist Millicent Garrett Fawcett.
8 Guru Nanak (1469-1539).
9 He was murdered at the outbreak of the Spanish Civil War.
10 The Soviet writers Ilf and Petrov.
11 Sir William Herschel.
12 Dionysius I of Syracuse.
13 Gabriel Rossetti (1783-1854), Christina Georgina (1830-94), Dante Gabriel (1828-82), William Michael (1829-1919).
14 Theology.
15 Queen Victoria.

1 Molière.
2 Siddhartha Gautama.
3 They were a prolific Swiss family of mathematicians and scientists.
4 Botany.
5 Woodford.
6 Anne Mansfield Sullivan.
7 Mexican.
8 John Hanning Speke. He discovered it in 1858.
9 Ralph David Abernathy from 1968-77.
10 William Huskisson.
11 Thomas Masaryk from 1918-1935.
12 Anwar Sadat, Menahem Begin and Jimmy Carter as witness.
13 Galba, Otho, Vitellius, Vespasian.
14 After her native Melbourne; her real name was Helen Armstrong, (née Mitchell).
15 Agrippina.

1 George Escoffier.
2 Julius Martov.
3 Edward Kennedy.
4 Ludwik Zamenhov.
5 Edward Teller.
6 Valentina Tereshkova in 1963.
7 Cornelia, Pompeia and Calpurnia.
8 Currer Bell (Charlotte), Ellis Bell (Emily), Acton Bell (Anne).
9 John Donne.
10 Theodore Roosevelt. He took office at the age of 42.
11 Mary Ann Evans and Mary Ann Cross.
12 Sir John Vanbrugh.
13 Aristide Briand and Gustav Stresemann.
14 In the same order: Russell, Cavendish, Fitzalan Howard,
and Grosvenor.
15 He wore a kilt.

1 William Joyce.
2 Gavrilo Princip.
3 Edward V and Edward VIII.
4 Viscount Castlereagh and Getúlio Vargas.
5 The Iceni.
6 Clifford, Ashley, Buckingham, Arlington and Lauderdale.
7 He was the grandson of John of Gaunt.
8 The Earl of Liverpool.
9 Gordon Lonsdale.
10 Henry IV from 1589-1610.
11 Clark Gable.
12 William Holman Hunt, John Everett Millais, D.G. Rossetti, James Collinson, F.G. Stephens,
Thomas Woolner and W.M.Rossetti.
13 Modern chemistry.
14 They all qualified as doctors.
15 Mehmed VI from 1918-22.

PEOPLE **ANSWERS**

1 Viscount Stansgate.
2 Theobald von Bethmann Hollweg.
3 Joseph Grimaldi.
4 Jawaharlal Nehru, Lal Bahadur Shastri and Indira Gandhi.
5 Raymond Poincaré.
6 Michael Romanov - from 1613-1645.
7 Jacques Cartier - in 1534.
8 Countess Markiewicz in 1918.
9 Theodoric the Great.
10 Samuel Coleridge - Taylor (1875-1912).
11 He entered a Conservative, became an Indepent and then represented the Labour Party.
12 Arthur Wesley - later Arthur Wellesley.
13 A. Lincoln in 1865, J.A. Garfield in 1881, W. McKinley in 190l,
J.F. Kennedy in 1963.
14 Robert Dudley, Earl of Leicester.
15 They were Dr Crippen's wife and mistress.

1 Herodotus.
2 Malcolm X.
3 Hatshepsut.
4 Joseph Vissarionovich Dzhugashvili, Vladimir Ilyich Ulyanov and Lev Davydovich Brontstein.
5 Edward III.
6 Georgi Malenkov.
7 Willi Stoph.
8 The Duke of Berwick. He received the title Marshal of France.
9 Jean Henri Dunant, after witnessing the Battle of Solferino in 1859.
10 When as a youth he danced the part of the sun in *Ballet de la nuit*.
11 Don Carlo Gesualdo.
12 Saint Geneviève. She saved the city from conquest by the Huns in AD 451.
13 John Flamsteed from 1675-1719.
14 A 17th century Italian painter and exponent of the style of Caravaggio.
15 Antoine Lavoisier.

1 Romulus Augustulus.
2 Wrapping and labeling pots in a blacking factory - aged 12.
3 Byron, according to Lady Caroline Lamb.
4 Churchill, Lord Beaverbrook and John Simon.
5 Sam Nujoma.
6 Sir Walter Scott.
7 Benedict Spinoza.
8 Margrethe II.
9 Saint Thomas Aquinas.
10 Warren Hastings.
11 James Callaghan.
12 Lucius Septimius Severus, c146-211 AD.
13 Georg Cantor.
14 Ulrich Zwingli.
15 Maksim Gorki.

1 Tafari Makonnen.
2 Anne of Cleves.
3 Alice Liddel - daughter of the Dean of Christ Church.
4 Dame Alicia Markova.
5 The Fates.
6 Charles Chaplin, Douglas Fairbanks, Mary Pickford (and director D.W. Griffith).
7 Cicero.
8 Ivan the Terrible.
9 The Marquess of Salisbury - Prime Minister three times: 1885-6; 1886-92; 1895-1902.
10 Syracuse, Sicily.
11 A Danish historian of the 12th - 13th centuries.
12 Roald Amundsen in 1903-6. He was the first completely to traverse the passage by ship.
13 A ruler of ancient Britain known to literature as Cymbeline.
14 Sir Joshua Reynolds.
15 Marcus Garvey.

1 Eamon De Valera in 1926. It means 'soldiers of destiny'.
2 Sir James Brooke in 1841.
3 Benjamin Franklin.
4 Prince George of Denmark.
5 Calixtus III (Alfonso Borgia) and Alexander VI (Rodrigo Borgia).
6 A theory of evolution which was superseded by the works of Charles Darwin.
7 Lorenzo Da Ponte.
8 William Sydney Porter.
9 Wyndham Lewis.
10 R. Buckminster Fuller.
11 Garibaldi during the conquest of Southern Italy.
12 Nathuram Godse.
13 Leipzig.
14 Ovid for immorality.
15 Euripides.

1 In which centuries were Buddhism and Islam founded?

2 Who headed the government of Hungary during the 1956 uprising, but was arrested after Soviet intervention and later executed?

3 Which Holy Roman Emperor's troops 'sacked' Rome in 1527?

4 What was the 'Ausgleich'?

5 What happended at Actium in 31 BC?

6 Who was the first European to sail around the southern tip of Africa?

7 What were Germany's African colonies at the outbreak of World War I?

8 Which English MP had engraved on his coffin 'a Friend to Liberty'?

9 Who were 'Too frightened to fight each other; too stupid to agree'?

10 Who was the US President at the time of the Wall Street Crash?

11 What momentous event took place on a University of Chicago squash court?

12 Which religious conflict is associated with the Byzantine Emperor Leo III the Isaurian?

13 Who was shot "pour encourager les autres"?

14 Who summoned the Model Parliament?

15 Which education minister inaugurated a system of universal secondary education in Britain in 1944?

EVENTS QUESTIONS

1 Who was the Old Pretender?

2 Where and when was the 'Revolution of Flowers'?

3 Why was the statue in Paris respresenting Strasbourg shrouded from 1871-1918?

4 Who were the Fatimids?

5 In which years were the Suez and Panama Canals opened?

6 Which treaty in 1648 concluded the Thirty Years' War?

7 What was the Defenestration of Prague?

8 Who was the last great Zulu king, who was defeated by the British in 1879?

9 Which edict declared Martin Luther an outlaw and heretic?

10 Which Labour minister resigned in 1930 over the issue of unemployment?

11 At which conference in 1944 was the IMF founded?

12 Between World Wars I and II, which countries formed the Little Entente?

13 Which US Congressional action of 1964 was called 'the functional equivalent of a declaration of war'?

14 In British history what did the years 1832, 1867 and 1884 have in common?

15 What and where was the Mannerheim Line?

1 Who was the first president of Nigeria?

2 Which Bolshevik newspaper was founded in April 1912?

3 In whose reign was Monmouth's Rebellion?

4 Who became president of a newly independent African country in 1957, was appointed president for life in 1975 and is still president?

5 Who commanded the Russian forces against Napoleon at the battle of Borodino?

6 Who was the world's first woman Prime Minister? ✓

7 Which woman united Norway, Denmark and Sweden in the 14th century?

8 Who was the last king of ancient Rome?

9 Why did civil war break out in England in 1139?

10 Which Holy Roman Emperor drowned during the Third Crusade?

11 Who was the hero of Porto Bello in 1739?

12 Who was the French 'citizen King'?

13 In which year did the Pilgrim Fathers land in America?

14 In which country was the independence party Istiqlal founded in 1943?

15 What was the Zollverein?

1 Who was the founding father of Pakistan?

2 Which religious movement was inspired by a mystical experience in Aldersgate Street, London, in 1738?

3 Who were the original five members of Churchill's war cabinet?

4 When was the Boxer Uprising?

5 At which battle was Joan of Arc captured and by whom?

6 Who commanded the Spanish Armada?

7 In which decade was the office of doge of Venice abolished?

8 Who sacked Moscow in 1382?

9 Where and when was the TUC founded?

10 Which European country lost two-thirds of its territory by the Treaty of Trianon in 1920?

11 Where was the first A-bomb exploded?

12 In which war was the battle of Navarino fought in 1827, and why was it the last of its kind?

13 Which was the first country to give women the vote? ✓

14 Who founded the Achaemenid (Persian) Empire?

15 Where and what was the Meiji Period?

1 Which dynasty of former slave-soldiers ruled Egypt and Syria from 1250-1517?

2 When was the Great Peloponnesian War fought and who won it?

3 In which country did a population of approximately eight million in 1840, halve by 1910?

4 Who said: "We must be the great arsenal of democracy"?

5 In the American Civil war, where did General Robert E. Lee surrender to General Ulysses S. Grant?

6 What was the full German name of the Nazi Party?

7 Name the last five popes.

8 Which Archbishop of Canterbury was executed during the English Civil War in 1645?

9 Who was the captain-general of the New Model army at the battle of Naseby in 1645?

10 What is the origin of the word 'fascism'?

11 Which Portuguese king lived and died in Twickenham?

12 Which US Presidents signed the Constitution?

13 What name was given to the Japanese puppet state established in Manchuria from 1932-45?

14 Where did Churchill, Roosevelt and Stalin meet?

15 What was the Kellogg-Briand Pact?

1 What does the Titus Arch in Rome commemorate?

2 Which country abolished the fez in 1925 and under which ruler?

3 In which year was VAT introduced in Britain?

4 Who was known as 'The master-thief of the unknown world'?

5 Over which issue was the last referendum held in Britain?

6 For what is Colonel Thomas Pride chiefly remembered?

7 Where did the Long March end?

8 Who was described as 'the only man who could lose World War I in an afternoon'?

9 Who fought whom at Orongomai in 1860?

10 Whose empire in 1227 stretched from Peking to the Caspian Sea?

11 Which play was Abraham Lincoln watching when he was assassinated?

12 How did Britain acquire the island of Hong Kong?

13 In which city did the poet Gabriele D'Annunzio proclaim 'the Italian regency of the Carnaro' in 1920?

14 Who founded the Pahlavi dynasty in Iran?

15 What was the date and the place of the formal German surrender in World War II?

1 What were the first and second Reichs?

2 Where - on December 29th 1890 - was the white conquest of American Indians completed?

3 Which pope called the First Crusade?

4 When did Belgium become independent?

5 What was the last of President Wilson's Fourteen Points?

6 Who was Secretary General of the UN during the Suez crisis?

7 Which two people were awarded the Nobel peace prize for negotiating the Vietnam cease-fire agreement of 1973?

8 Who was the last Manchu emperor of China?

9 Which two countries signed the treaty of Unkiar Skelessi in 1833 and for which secret clause was it significant?

10 Which was the first empire to rule most of India?

11 Who was German supreme commander in western Europe at the time of the D-Day Normandy Invasion?

12 When were women given equal voting rights to men in the UK?

13 In 1964 Ghana became a one-party state under Kwame Nkrumah. Which party did he lead?

14 When did the US acquire the Philippines?

15 Which historic meeting took place in a scruffy house at 30 Holford Square, Kings Cross, in October 1902?

1 What were the last three Chinese dynasties?

2 Who founded the Mogul Empire?

3 Which king of England was born in Pembroke Castle?

4 Which two brothers led the first Anglo-Saxon settlement of Britain?

5 Who led the Norfolk rebellion of 1549?

6 Which Ottoman sultan conquered Belgrade in 1521, Rhodes in 1522, defeated the Hungarians but failed to win Vienna?

7 To what did Lord Lothian refer in the 1930s when he said: "After all, they are only going into their own back garden"?

8 Who was the last emperor of Austria?

9 Which Central American countries fought a war over a football match in 1969?

10 Who was the first person to sign the American Declaration of Independence?

11 In World War II, where was the Gothic Line?

12 Which statute of 1931 granted political autonomy to the dominions?

13 Of which 19th century movement were William Lovett and Feargus O'Connor leading figures?

14 What was the 'Popish Plot' and who fabricated it?

15 Who succeeded Mao Tse-tung as chairman of the Chinese Communist Party and Chou En-lai as premier?

1 Who was the first king of a united Italy?

2 Who assassinated Jean-Paul Marat?

3 At which conference was the United Nations charter drafted?

4 Who founded the Spanish Falange?

5 Who were the members of the First and Second Triumvirates in Rome?

6 Which South African Prime Minister was assassinated in 1966?

7 Which British Prime Minister was assassinated?

8 Who said: "Italy is a geographical expression"?

9 Which Anglo-Saxon kingdom was created through the union of Bernicia and Deira?

10 What name is given to the 1536 rebellion in the reign of Henry VIII led by Robert Aske?

11 Place in chronological order: Peasants' Revolt, Wars of the Roses, Death of Kublai Khan, Children's Crusade.

12 Who founded the Grand National Consolidated Trades Union?

13 Which African leader became president of his country in 1971 and was overthrown by a coup in April 1985?

14 When did the battle of Rivoli take place and who won it?

15 In 1534, where did the Anabaptists found their 'Kingdom of 1000 years'?

1 What was the Glorious Revolution?

2 Who met whom on the Field of the Cloth of Gold?

3 Who was the first woman to join a British cabinet?

4 How many US vice presidents since 1945 have become president?

5 What was the Edict of Nantes and who revoked it?

6 Whose mistress was Madame de Pompadour?

7 What events marked the beginning and end of the French Second Republic?

8 What were 'Guelfs' and 'Ghibellines'?

9 Who were the Roman emperors at the time of the Nativity and the Crucifixion?

10 At which battle was Henry Percy (Hotspur) killed?

11 Who was chancellor of the exchequer when premium bonds were introduced in 1956?

12 What were the Gordon Riots?

13 Who led the first overland expedition across America from St. Louis to the North Pacific Ocean and back?

14 Which was the last dynasty of Japanese shoguns?

15 Who instituted the Papal Inquisition in 1231?

1 Where did General Gordon die?

2 Which Health Minister was responsible for establishing the National Health Service?

3 Which was the first American State to secede from the Union?

4 In which war did Britain capture Gibraltar?

5 According to convention in which years did the Hundred Years' War begin and end?

6 Who were the last three Liberals to be Prime Ministers of Britain?

7 Including the Eastern Empire, how long did the Roman Empire survive?

8 To what did the term 'Fifth Column' originally refer?

9 Who were the rulers of Malta between 1530 and 1798?

10 Which crusade did Innocent III launch against Catharist heretics?

11 Which countries withdrew their forces from NATO command in 1966 and 1974?

12 Why was Stalin presented with a sword in 1943 as a gift from the king of England?

13 Which country controlled Hormuz in the 16th Century?

14 What name is given to Bismarck's struggle to place the Catholic church under state control?

15 What were 'Potemkin villages'?

1 In which year did Mussolini seize power?

2 In which battle and in which war did which sovereign become the last British king to lead his troops in the field?

3 Who was the first Prime Minister of Bangladesh, who was assassinated in 1975?

4 Which was the first country to prohibit the slave trade?

5 Which four leaders drew up the Munich Agreement?

6 In which century was the Ming Dynasty founded?

7 How long did the General Strike last?

8 In World War II what were 'Torch', 'Husky' and 'Overlord'?

9 Name the next five kings of England after William the Conqueror.

10 Which countries fought the Chaco War?

11 When did the United Kingdom of Great Britain and Ireland come into existence?

12 Which services were merged in 1918 to form the RAF?

13 Who were the last two Communist Party MPs in Britain?

14 Who is called the 'father of Russian Marxism'?

15 What is Marinus van der Lubbe's claim to fame?

1 What was Enosis?

2 What was the main business for which the South Sea Company was set up?

3 Which leaders signed the SALT 1 agreements?

4 Where did the two famous naval mutinies of April and May 1797 take place?

5 Who were the runners-up in the elections of presidents Johnson and Nixon?

6 Which countries were involved in the Fashoda incident?

7 Who was the formal head of the Soviet State from 1919-46?

8 In 1919, who made the first non-stop flight across the Atlantic?

9 Which people under which king sacked Rome in AD 410?

10 In 1960, who led the secession of Katanga province from the newly independent Congo?

11 Who was commander-in-chief of the French army during the first battle of the Marne?

12 Which Tsar emancipated the serfs?

13 Name two of the founders of the Spartacus League.

14 Which Appollo mission completed the first manned lunar landing, which three astronauts were involved, and when?

15 Who were awarded the Victoria Cross for service in the Falklands War?

EVENTS **ANSWERS**

1 6th century BC and 7th century AD.
2 Imre Nagy.
3 Charles V's.
4 The "compromise" of 1867 that created the dual monarchy of Austria-Hungary.
5 Octavian defeated Mark Antony to become master of the Roman world.
6 Bartolomeu Dias in 1488.
7 German East Africa, German South West Africa, Cameroons and Togo.
8 John Wilkes 1725-97.
9 The allies at the Congress of Vienna (1814-15).
10 Herbert Hoover.
11 The world's first controlled nuclear chain reaction, in 1942.
12 The Iconoclastic Controversy. He officially prohibited the use of icons in AD 730.
13 Admiral Byng - inspiring Voltaire's remark that the English occasionally shoot an admiral "to encourage the others".
14 Edward I in 1295.
15 R.A. Butler.

1 James Edward Stuart, son of James II and claimant to the English and Scottish thrones.
2 Portugal in 1974.
3 Strasbourg was captured by Germany during the Franco-Prussian War and recovered by France in 1918.
4 A Muslim dynasty that established a medieval empire in N. Africa, the Middle East and Sicily.
5 1869 and 1914.
6 The Peace of Westphalia.
7 The ejection from a window of two imperial regents by Bohemian Protestants, which helped spark off the Thirty Years' War.
8 Cetshwayo.
9 The Edict of Worms (1521).
10 Sir Oswald Mosley.
11 The Bretton Woods Conference.
12 Czechoslovakia, Romania and Yugoslavia.
13 The Gulf of Tonkin Resolution (the response to a Vietnamese attack on American ships)which 'authorised' military action by the US in Vietnam.
14 They were all years of Reform Acts.
15 A Finnish defence line facing Russia during World War II.

1 Sir Abubakar Tafawa Balewa.
2 *Pravda.*
3 James II's.
4 Habib Bourguiba of Tunisia.
5 General Kutuzov.
6 Mrs Bandaranaike of Sri Lanka (formerly Ceylon) who took office in 1960.
7 Margaret of Denmark, Norway and Sweden.
8 Lucius Tarquinius Superbus, from 534-510 BC.
9 Over rival claims to the throne by Stephen and Matilda.
10 Frederick I (Barbarossa) 1121-90.
11 Admiral Vernon, who captured the Spanish settlement using only six ships during the War of Jenkins' Ear.
12 Louis-Philippe.
13 1620.
14 Morocco.
15 A customs union of German states founded in 1834.

4

1 Mohammed Ali Jinnah.
2 Methodism - the experience was John Wesley's.
3 Churchill, Chamberlain, Lord Halifax, Attlee and Arthur Greenwood.
4 1900.
5 Compiègne in 1430, by the Burgundians who sold her to their allies, the English.
6 The Duke of Medina Sidonia.
7 The 1790s (1797) during Napoleon's conquest of N. Italy.
8 Tokhtamysh - Khan of the Golden Horde.
9 Manchester in 1868.
10 Hungary.
11 Alamogordo, New Mexico in 1945.
12 The Greek War of Independence. It was the last major battle fought under sail.
13 New Zealand in 1893.
14 Cyrus the Great.
15 The period from 1868-1912 in Japan when the country was modernised under Emperor Mutsuhito who received the title 'Meiji' ('enlightened ruler').

1 The Mamelukes.
2 431-404 BC. Sparta defeated Athens.
3 Ireland.
4 F.D. Roosevelt.
5 Appomattox Court House - in 1865.
6 Nationalsozialistische Deutsche Arbeiterpartei.
7 Pius XII (1939-58), John XXIII (1958-63), Paul VI (1963-78), John Paul I (1978) and John Paul II (1978 -).
8 William Laud.
9 Thomas Fairfax.
10 From the Latin *fasces* ('bundles') - denoting a bundle of elm or birch rods containing an axe - an ancient Roman sign of authority. Mussolini adopted the symbol in 1919.
11 Manuel II - the last Portuguese king, in exile.
12 Washington and Madison.
13 Manchukuo.
14 The Teheran Conference in 1943 and the Yalta Conference in 1945.
15 A formal agreement to renouce war as an instrument of national policy signed by over sixty states between the two World Wars.

1 The Roman conquest of Jerusalem in AD 70.
2 Turkey, under Kemal Ataturk.
3 1973.
4 Francis Drake.
5 Devolution, in 1979.
6 Pride's Purge - the expulsion of MPs from the Long Parliament in 1648 that left behind the 'Rump'.
7 Yen-an, in Shensi Province.
8 Admiral Jellicoe.
9 The forces of the New Zealand colonists fought and defeated the Maoris.
10 Genghis Khan's.
11 *Our American Cousin* by Tom Taylor.
12 It was ceded to Britain as a result of the first Opium War. The other parts of Hong Kong were acquired later.
13 Fiume (Rijeka) - now in Yugoslavia.
14 Reza Shah Pahlavi in 1925.
15 7th May 1945 at Reims.

1 The Holy Roman Empire was the first. The German Empire 1871-1918 was the second.
2 At Wounded Knee.
3 Pope Urban II.
4 1831.
5 The setting up of a general association of nations.
6 Dag Hammarskjöld.
7 Henry Kissinger and Le Duc Tho (who declined to accept it).
8 Henry Pu-yi (Hsüan-T'ung). He abdicated in 1912.
9 Russia and Turkey. Turkey agreed to close the Dardanelles to foreign warships at Russia's request, in the event of war.
10 The Mauryan Empire - c321-185 BC.
11 Field Marshall von Rundstedt.
12 1928.
13 The Convention People's Party.
14 In 1898 after the Spanish American War.
15 The first meeting of Lenin and Trotsky.

1 Yüan (Mongol), Ming and Ch'ing (Manchu).
2 Baber, in 1526.
3 Henry VII.
4 Hengist and Horsa - according to legend.
5 Robert Kett.
6 Suleiman the Magnificent.
7 German military occupation of the demilitarised zone of the Rhineland.
8 Charles I, from 1916-18. He was also Charles IV king of Hungary.
9 Honduras and El Salvador.
10 John Hancock.
11 It was the final German defence line in Italy, running north of Florence across the peninsula.
12 Statute of Westminster.
13 Chartism.
14 Allegations by Titus Oates in 1678 of a Roman Catholic conspiracy to seize power.
15 Hua Kuo-feng.

1 Victor Emmanuel II.
2 Charlotte Corday.
3 The San Francisco Conference in 1945.
4 José Antonio Primo de Rivera.
5 Caesar, Pompey and Crassus (the so-called first) and Mark Antony, Lepidus and Octavian (the second).
6 Hendrik Frensch Verwoerd - in Parliament.
7 Spencer Perceval in 1812.
8 Metternich.
9 Northumbria.
10 The Pilgrimage of Grace.
11 Children's Crusade 1212, Death of Kublai Khan 1294, Peasants' Revolt 1381 and Wars of the Roses 1455-85.
12 Robert Owen.
13 President Nimeiry of the Sudan.
14 1797 Napoleon defeated the Austrians.
15 Münster.

1 The ousting of James II and the accession of Mary II and her husband William of Orange as constitutional monarchs.
2 Henry VIII met Francis I of France in 1520.
3 Margaret Bondfield - as minister of labour in 1929 under Ramsey MacDonald.
4 Four. Truman, Johnson, Nixon and Ford.
5 A decree (1598) of Henry IV of France that gave religious freedom to the Huguenots. It was revoked by Louis XIV in 1685.
6 Louis XV's.
7 The revolution of 1848 when Louis Philippe was overthrown, and Louis Napoleon (the president) declaring himself emperor in 1852.
8 The two great political factions of medieval Italy during the struggle between the Empire and the Papacy. The Guelfs were the papal faction and the Ghibellines supported the Holy Roman Emperors.
9 Augustus and Tiberius.
10 The battle of Shrewsbury in 1403.
11 Harold Macmillan.
12 Serious anti-Catholic riots instigated by Lord George Gordon in 1780.
13 Meriwether Lewis and William Clark 1804-6.
14 The Tokugawa (1603-1867).
15 Pope Gregory IX.

EVENTS ANSWERS

1 At the siege of Khartoum, Sudan in 1885.
2 Aneurin Bevan in 1946.
3 South Carolina in 1860.
4 The War of the Spanish Succession.
5 1337-1453.
6 Sir Henry Campbell-Bannerman, H.H. Asquith and Lloyd George (who headed a coalition).
7 1480 years - from the accession of Augustus in 27 BC until the fall of Constantinople in 1453.
8 It referred to Nationalist supporters behind Loyalist lines in Madrid when the city was being advanced upon by four Nationalist columns during the Spanish Civil War.
9 The Knights of Saint John of Jerusalem (the Hospitallers).
10 The Albigensian Crusade.
11 France, and Greece (over the Turkish invasion of Cyprus).
12 As a tribute to Russian heroism at Stalingrad.
13 Portugal from 1514-1622.
14 Kulturkampf.
15 Artificial villages erected by Potemkin to fool Catherine the Great.

1 1922 after the 'March on Rome'.
2 The battle of Dettingen, the War of the Austrian Succession and King George II.
3 Sheikh Mujibur Rahman.
4 Denmark in 1792.
5 Adolf Hitler, Neville Chamberlain, Benito Mussolini and Edouard Daladier.
6 14th century.
7 Nine days.
8 Allied invasions of N.W. Africa, Sicily and Normandy.
9 William II, Henry I, Stephen, Henry II and Richard I.
10 Bolivia and Paraguay in the 1930s.
11 January 1st 1801.
12 Royal Naval Air Service and Royal Flying Corps.
13 Willie Gallagher and Phil Piratin from 1945-1950.
14 Georgi Plekhanov.
15 He set fire to the Reichstag in 1933.

1 The political movement for the union of Cyprus and Greece.
2 Slave-trading.
3 Richard Nixon (USA) and Leonid Brezhnev (USSR).
4 At Spithead and the Nore.
5 Barry Goldwater, Hubert Humphrey.
6 Britain and France.
7 Mikhail Kalinin.
8 Alcock and Brown.
9 The Visigoths under Alaric I.
10 Moise Tshombe.
11 General Joffre.
12 Alexander II in 1861.
13 Rosa Luxemburg, Karl Liebknecht, Clara Zetkin and Franz Mehring.
14 Appollo 11 Neil Armstrong, Edwin Aldrin and Michael Collins, 20th July 1969.
15 Lt. Col. Herbert Jones and Sgt. Ian John McKay.

DISCOVERY & INVENTION QUESTIONS 1

1 What is the chemical formula for ozone?

2 What shape is the DNA molecule?

3 What are the shortest electromagnetic waves of terrestrial origin?

4 Who designed the VW Beetle?

5 What is the instrument that measures blood pressure called?

6 What is the Doppler effect?

7 For what was Otto Hahn awarded the Nobel prize for chemistry?

8 Who built the first four-stroke internal combustion engine?

9 For what is 'Y' the chemical symbol?

10 What is the function of a diode in electronic circuits?

11 What is a parsec?

12 What name is given to the group of elements which include fluorine, chlorine, bromine and iodine?

13 Of which element is tritium an isotope?

14 Which substance escaped to cause the 1984 Bhopal catastrophe?

15 What is crocidolite and why is it dangerous?

1 What is sometimes known as the Fourth State of Matter?

2 For what is BASIC an acronym?

3 Which heart drug derives from foxglove?

4 For what invention is Jethro Tull famous?

5 What is invar?

6 Who were the three main scientists involved in the discovery of oxygen?

7 Who first vulcanized rubber?

8 Who discovered radioactivity?

9 Which dietary deficiency causes pernicious anaemia?

10 What do histologists study?

11 Which discovery in 1900, and by whom, made blood transfusions safer?

12 Who won a prize of 12,000 francs for inventing a method of food preservation during the Napoleonic Wars?

13 What approximately, is the half-life of the radioactive isotope plutonium-239?

14 Who wrote *The Structure of Scientific Revolutions*?

15 What is the Crookes dark space?

1 Who is generally credited with the invention of the piano?

2 Which two gases are normally used to fill fluorescent tubes?

3 Who designed the Mini and the Morris Minor?

4 Which famous weaving invention was patented by John Kay in 1733?

5 What is Ohm's law?

6 What does aqua regia - which can dissolve gold - contain?

7 What is a lux?

8 What was Watt's main contribution to steam technology?

9 Which vitamin is particularly important for blood clotting?

10 What is a henry?

11 Rhombic, monoclinic and plastic are forms of which element?

12 Who are the two mathematicians credited with the invention of calculus?

13 What is the most electronegative element?

14 Which two scientists shared the Nobel prize with Fleming for work on penicillin?

15 Approximately how often does Neptune orbit the sun?

1 How many chromosomes are there in a normal human body cell?

2 What was the first spacecraft to be launched into orbit for the second time?

3 What is Kwok's disease?

4 What was the first sub-atomic particle to be discovered?

5 Name five of the six noble gases.

6 What was the first truly automatic machine-gun?

7 What is splanchnology?

8 For what is the late Vladimir Zworykin known?

9 Who discovered the tuberculosis bacterium?

10 Who founded osteopathy?

11 What was Lee De Forest's major contribution to technology?

12 Which two letters have not been used in the periodic table?

13 What is tribophysics?

14 What is the unit of electrical conductance?

15 What is the Haber process?

1 What are the main constituents of acid rain? ✓

2 What do RNA and DNA stand for?

3 How many faces has a dodecahedron?

4 What is the chemical formula for caustic soda?

5 Which scientist discovered that citrus fruit could prevent scurvy?

6 Who discovered the neutron?

7 What is an ion?

8 What is the significance of 9,192,631,770 cycles of caesium vibration?

9 Who wrote the *Sceptical Chymist*?

10 Who was regarded as the supreme medical and anatomical authority from the 2nd century AD until the Renaissance?

11 Which element has the atomic number 101?

12 Who built the first practical typewriter?

13 What is a Fibonacci series?

14 Which two scientists won the 1909 Nobel prize for work on wireless telegraphy?

15 Which 1881 experiment paved the way for Einstein's theory of relativity, because of what it didn't prove?

1 Who discovered polonium?

2 What is a pulsar?

3 What is a cytometer?

4 What is considered to be Sir Isaac Newton's greatest published work?

5 What is turpentine made from?

6 Who is credited with the discovery of the relationship between electricity and magnetism?

7 What are isotopes?

8 In micro-electronics, what do the letters VLSI stand for?

9 In which decade was the electrocardiograph invented?

10 What, approximately, is the melting point of the metal gallium?

11 Who invented the vacuum flask?

12 Which chemical substance has a form known as plaster of paris?

13 What was the first effective treatment for syphilis and who developed it?

14 What is a Ringelmann chart used for?

15 What is the full chemical name of the herbicide 2,4,5-T ?

1 Who sent rockets to bomb London and man to the moon?

2 Who discovered the circulation of blood?

3 Who invented nylon?

4 Who discovered the elliptical nature of planetary orbits?

5 What is the lowest temperature theoretically possible?

6 Who founded modern eugenics?

7 What is a tachyon?

8 What was the first virus to be isolated?

9 What is the device used to produce microwaves in domestic microwave cooking appliances?

10 Approximately what temperature is attained in oxy-acetylene welding?

11 Which mother and daughter won Nobel prizes for science?

12 What is the modified Mercalli scale used for?

13 What is Maxwell's Demon?

14 What is the generic name given to the chemicals used in aerosols that are thought to cause damage to the ozone layer?

15 What is the international Morse code for 'S.O.S.' ?

1 What is the lightest metal?

2 What is a plasmodium?

3 Who discovered the basic laws of genetics while working with peas in a monastery garden?

4 What is pinchbeck?

5 What is dendrochronology?

6 Who first provided evidence that the universe is expanding?

7 Of what is Andreas Vesalius called the 'father'?

8 Which smokeless explosive did Abel and Dewar invent in the late 1880s?

9 What does the symbol 'h' represent to a physicist?

10 What is the electrolyte in zinc-carbon battery cells?

11 What does DDT stand for?

12 What type of fuel is normally used in jet aircraft engines?

13 Who invented the photocopying machine?

14 What is a superfluid?

15 Who invented portland cement?

1 Of what substances was the first gunpowder (black powder) made?

2 Excluding the Earth, how many planets were known by the year 1800?

3 Which famous discovery did Michael Faraday make in 1831?

4 What name is given to the unit of distance equal to a ten thousand millionth of a metre?

5 Who invented the hovercraft?

6 For what achievement was Albert Einstein awarded the Nobel prize?

7 Of what is the gauss a unit?

8 Which other disease is said to be caused by the chicken pox virus?

9 Who discovered the uncertainty principle?

10 What is the principal use of germanium?

11 In which discipline was Sir Charles Lyell an influential figure?

12 What is Boyle's law?

13 Who was the first director of the Cavendish Laboratory?

14 In computer terminology, what is a PROM?

15 Which important medical breakthrough involved the dye Prontosil Red?

1 What was the theory proposed by James Jeans and argued by Sir Fred Hoyle in opposition to the 'big bang' theory?

2 What is the literal meaning of 'to vaccinate'?

3 Who discovered X-rays?

4 Who invented the first practical steam engine?

5 Who invented the capillary feed fountain pen?

6 Of what is C_2H_5OH the formula?

7 What acronym was given to the world's first electronic digital computer?

8 What physical phenomenon was finally proved possible in 1650 by Otto von Guericke?

9 Which chemical element - atomic number 100 - is named after a 20th century Italian physicist?

10 In astrophysics, what is a singularity?

11 What does MASER stand for?

12 How do you make a metal superconductive?

13 Why was the invention of the chronometer so important in the history of navigation?

14 What is stereochemistry?

15 Who invented the aqualung?

1 Who invented the cotton gin?

2 What is the significance of 101,325 pascals?

3 For developing which device - used to study the behaviour of sub-atomic particles - was Donald Glaser awarded the Nobel prize?

4 From which mineral ore can mercury be obtained simply by heating?

5 On whose work is the modern periodic classification of elements based?

6 In computer science, how many bytes are there in a kilobyte of memory?

7 Which of the following are polymers: starch, rubber, sugar, cellulose, graphite?

8 Who first accurately measured the speed of light, and in which decade?

9 What is a perfect number?

10 Who are the inventors of the transistor?

11 Who produced the first permanent photographic image?

12 What was the first spacecraft to reach the surface of the moon?

13 What is the unit of electrical capacitance?

14 What does the prefix 'nano-' mean in scientific measurement?

15 What does the atomic number of an element represent?

1 At what temperature do the Celsius and Fahrenheit scales converge?

2 What is the modern chemical name for the antiseptic substance carbolic?

3 Who invented the compound microscope?

4 What was the safety device invented by Percy Shaw in 1934?

5 Soap is probably the oldest chemical invention. How could a cave-person have made it?

6 Who developed the first effective vaccine against polio?

7 Who originated quantum theory?

8 What is an imaginary number?

9 Which is the main metal additive used to make steel stainless?

10 What is the product of a volt and an amp?

11 What caused the destruction of the Tacoma Narrows Bridge in 1940?

12 Of what common household substance is CH_3COOH a constituent?

13 What was the first transuranium element to be discovered?

14 What is a Kipp's apparatus used for?

15 What method did Humphrey Davy use to discover sodium and potassium?

1 What is 'dry ice'?

2 What is the third most common element in the Earth's crust - of which sapphire and ruby are compounds?

3 What is the name of the process by which soft fats and oils are hardened to produce margarine?

4 Who won the 1923 Nobel prize for discovering insulin?

5 What does TNT stand for?

6 What are the two chemical constituents of the synthetic material Bakelite?

7 What is polytetrafluoroethylene commonly known as?

8 Who discovered the electron?

9 What are these: FBR, PWR and AGR?

10 Who invented the stethoscope?

11 Who invented the mercury thermometer?

12 Who is credited with the invention of the vacuum cleaner?

13 Who invented float glass?

14 What is the literal meaning of the word 'atom'?

15 How did astronomers know of the existence of Neptune and Pluto before they were actually seen?

1 O_3.
2 A double helix.
3 Gamma rays.
4 Ferdinand Porsche.
5 Sphygmomanometer.
6 The change in frequency of waves (sound, light etc) from an object as it moves relative to the observer.
7 Research involving the splitting of the uranium atom.
8 Nikolaus Otto in 1876.
9 Yttrium.
10 It permits the flow of current in one direction only.
11 A unit of distance in astronomy equivalent to 19.2 million million miles.
12 The halogens.
13 Hydrogen.
14 Methyl isocyanate.
15 It is blue asbestos - the inhalation of which can cause asbestosis.

1 Plasma.
2 Beginners All Symbolic Instruction Code.
3 Digitalis.
4 The seed drill.
5 An alloy which exhibits negligible expansion on heating; used in precision mechanisms and measuring-standards.
6 Carl Scheele, Joseph Priestley, and Antoine Lavoisier who named it.
7 Charles Goodyear; his first patent was granted in 1844.
8 Henri Bequerel.
9 Lack of vitamin B12.
10 Animal and plant tissue.
11 The ABO blood groups by Karl Landsteiner.
12 Nicolas Appert - who first applied the technique of canning.
13 24,000 years.
14 Thomas Samuel Kuhn.
15 The non-luminous region often observed around the cathode of a gas-discharge tube.

1 Bartolommeo Cristofori in the early 18th century.
2 Argon and mercury vapour.
3 Sir Alexander Issigonis.
4 The flying shuttle.
5 The current in an electrical circuit is equal to the voltage across it divided by its resistance.
6 Approximately one part fuming nitric acid to three parts hydrochloric acid.
7 A unit of illumination.
8 He improved the Newcomen engine with a double-acting piston and a separate condenser.
9 Vitamin K.
10 A unit of electromagnetic inductance.
11 Sulphur.
12 Sir Isaac Newton and Gottfried Leibniz.
13 Fluorine.
14 H. W. Florey and Ernst Chain.
15 Every 165 years.

4

1 46.
2 The Columbia.
3 Allergy to monosodium glutamate.
4 The electron in 1895.
5 Helium, neon, argon, krypton, xenon, radon.
6 The Maxim gun, invented by Hiram Maxim in 1889.
7 The branch of anatomy concerned with the viscera - the internal organs.
8 Pioneering work on electronic image transmission on which modern television is based.
9 Robert Koch, in 1882.
10 Andrew T. Still.
11 He invented the triode valve - the first electronic amplifying device.
12 J and Q.
13 The physics of friction.
14 The mho.
15 An industrial process for the production of ammonia from its elements, hydrogen and nitrogen.

DISCOVERY & INVENTION ANSWERS

1 Acidic compounds of nitrogen and sulphur.

2 Ribonucleic acid and deoxyribonucleic acid.

3 Twelve.

4 NaOH.

5 James Lind. The Royal Navy adopted the practice of issuing citrus fruit to seamen at the end of the 18th century.

6 Sir James Chadwick in 1932.

7 An atom or group of atoms carrying a positive or negative electric charge.

8 It represents the international definition of a second.

9 Robert Boyle.

10 Galen of Pergamum.

11 Mendelevium.

12 Christopher Latham Sholes in 1868.

13 A number series in which each successive number is the sum of the previous two. E.g. 1, 1, 2, 3, 5, 8, 13...

14 Guglielmo Marconi and Karl Braun.

15 The Michelson-Morley experiment. Its failure to detect changes in the velocity of light due to the Earth's motion through the 'ether' caused the downfall of the ether theory thus making way for Einstein's theory of relativity.

---

1 Marie and Pierre Curie in 1898.

2 A pulsating radio star.

3 An apparatus for counting and measuring cells.

4 *The Principia Mathematica*.

5 The sap of the pine and other coniferous trees.

6 Hans Christian Oersted, in 1820.

7 Atoms of an element with the same atomic number but different atomic masses and physical properties.

8 Very Large Scale Integration.

9 The first decade of this century.

10 30°C.

11 Sir James Dewar in the 1890s.

12 Calcium sulphate.

13 Salvarsan, developed in 1909 by Paul Ehrlich.

14 Measuring the density of smoke by comparison of shades of grey.

15 2,4,5-trichlorophenoxyacetic acid.

1 Wernher von Braun. He developed the V-2 for Hitler and the Saturn V rockets used in the Apollo programme.
2 William Harvey, in the early 17th century.
3 Wallace Carothers.
4 Johannes Kepler.
5 0° K (Kelvin), equal to 273° C.
6 Sir Francis Galton.
7 A theoretical particle that travels faster than light.
8 Tobacco mosaic virus.
9 The magnetron.
10 3,250° C
11 Marie Curie and her daughter Irene Joliot-Curie.
12 Measuring the intensity of earthquakes.
13 An imaginary creature proposed by the physicist J.C. Maxwell which was theoretically capable of violating the second law of thermodynamics.
14 Fluorocarbons (freons).
15 Dot-dot-dot dash-dash-dash dot-dot-dot.

8

1 Lithium.
2 A single-celled parasitic organism responsible for malaria.
3 Gregor Mendel.
4 A cheap alloy of base metals (copper, zinc and tin) used as an imitation for gold.
5 The dating of past events through the study of annual tree rings.
6 Edwin Hubble in the 1920s - although as a theory it was not new.
7 Modern anatomy. His *Fabrica* of 1543 was the first proper description of human anatomy.
8 Cordite.
9 Planck's constant.
10 Ammonium chloride.
11 Dichloro-diphenyl-trichloroethane.
12 Paraffin (kerosene).
13 Chester F. Carlson who first patented the process in 1940.
14 A fluid cooled to near absolute zero, which exhibits very little friction and will flow up and over the sides of an open container.
15 Joseph Aspdin who filed his patent in 1824.

DISCOVERY & INVENTION ANSWERS

1 Saltpetre (potassium nitrate), carbon and sulphur.
2 Six: Mercury, Venus, Mars, Jupiter, Saturn and Uranus.
3 Electromagnetic induction.
4 An angstrom.
5 Sir Christopher Cockerell.
6 Discovery of the photoelectric effect and general services to theoretical physics.
7 Magnetic flux density.
8 Shingles.
9 Werner Heisenberg.
10 As an electronic semi-conductor.
11 Geology.
12 At a constant temperature the volume of a fixed mass of gas is inversely proportional to its pressure.
13 James Clerk Maxwell.
14 A programmable read only memory.
15 It was the material from which the first 'sulpha' drug - Prontosil - was made in the 1930s.

1 The steady state theory.
2 'To encow'. The term refers to the cowpox used by Edward Jenner in vaccinations for smallpox, 'vacca' meaning 'cow'.
3 Wilhelm Roentgen in 1895.
4 Thomas Newcomen, working on a design by Thomas Savery.
5 Lewis Waterman in 1884.
6 Ethyl alcohol.
7 ENIAC - Electronic numerical integrator and calculator.
8 The vacuum.
9 Fermium - after Enrico Fermi.
10 An anomaly in space-time, such as a black hole, where the classical laws of physics do not apply.
11 Microwave amplification by stimulated emission of radiation.
12 Cool it to a temperature approaching absolute zero.
13 It provided a means of accurately determining longitude.
14 The branch of chemistry concerned with the arrangement of the atoms of a molecule.
15 Jacques Cousteau.

1 Eli Whitney.
2 It is the average value of atmospheric pressure at sea level.
3 The bubble chamber.
4 Cinnabar (which contains mercuric sulphide).
5 Dimitrii Mendeleev.
6 1024.
7 Starch, rubber and cellulose.
8 Jean-Bernard Leon Foucault, in the 1850s.
9 A number which is the sum of its own factors.
10 William Shockley, John Bardeen and Walter Brattain in 1947.
11 Joseph Nièpce, in the 1820s.
12 The Soviet-built Luna II, in 1959.
13 The farad.
14 One-thousand-millionth-of.
15 The number of protons in the nucleus.

12

1 $-40°$.
2 Phenol.
3 Zacharias Janssen.
4 Road cat's-eye reflectors.
5 By boiling animal fats with alkalis obtained from wood ash.
6 Jonas Salk, first used in 1954
7 Max Planck.
8 The square root of a negative number. This is undefined, as the square of any number is always positive.
9 Chromium.
10 A watt.
11 Violent resonance of vibrations caused by wind.
12 Vinegar CH_3COOH is acetic acid.
13 Neptunium, in 1940.
14 Reactions in which a liquid is added to a solid to evolve a gas automatically - as and when required.
15 Electrolysis - the effect of an electric current on chemical compounds.

1 Solid carbon dioxide.
2 Aluminium.
3 Hydrogenation.
4 Sir F. G. Banting and J. J. R. Macleod.
5 Trinitrotoluene.
6 Formaldehyde and phenol.
7 'Teflon'.
8 J. J. Thomson.
9 Types of nuclear reactor: fast breeder reactor, pressurised water reactor and advanced gas-cooled reactor.
10 René Laënnec in 1816.
11 Daniel Fahrenheit in 1714.
12 Hubert Booth.
13 Alistair Pilkington in the 1950s.
14 'Indivisible' or 'uncut' - from the Greek.
15 Their gravitational forces caused perturbations in the orbits of their respective next inner planets.

NATURE QUESTIONS

1 Which animal secretes the pigment sepia?

2 A nictitating membrane is present in many vertebrates. What is it?

3 What are basenjis noted for?

4 Which group of animals is placed in the same order as rabbits and hares?

5 Why are frit flies a pest?

6 How do cocker spaniels get their name?

7 How many vertebrae are there in the human neck?

8 Between which dogs is the Boston terrier a cross?

9 What are the three families of living crocodilians?

10 What is the scientific term for the common potato?

11 What is the smallest mammal?

12 What are springtails?

13 Which animal has musth glands?

14 What is cassiterite?

15 What name is given to the motion caused by the Earth's rotation - by which winds and currents are deflected to the left in the southern hemisphere and to the right in the northern.

1 What are the largest and smallest living birds?

2 Which organism causes plague?

3 What is bladderwrack?

4 Which spice is obtained from the stigmas of the crocus?

5 Which animal is known as the glutton or skunk bear?

6 What is vitreous humour?

7 What are the two most abundant metallic elements in the human body?

8 What do the Haversian canals carry?

9 What are Dutch yellow long, Dutch red long, Magnum bonum and Shaw?

10 Of which wild animal is the chicken a domesticated form?

11 What dietary deficiency causes simple goitre?

12 Apart from its appearance, what is the hammerhead bird particularly noted for?

13 What is a nidifugous bird?

14 In which part of the body is the brachial artery?

15 How does the secretary bird get its name?

1 What is the specific food of leafcutter ants?

2 What colour are the flowers of the dill herb?

3 To which family do the apple and the plum belong?

4 How does the dachshund get its name?

5 Which living mammal is most closely related to the giraffe?

6 The axolotl is a highly unusual salamander. In what way?

7 Which part of the brain is chiefly responsible for balance and the co-ordination of muscular activity?

8 Which genus of trees provides the source of true gum arabic?

9 What is mitosis?

10 How does the archerfish get its name?

11 What is the largest order in the animal kingdom?

12 Of which well known mineral are pyrope and andradite varieties?

13 What is geotropism?

14 What is the anatomical name for the tear glands?

15 What is a fumarole?

1 What is the largest and heaviest organ in the human body?

2 What is a guanaco?

3 What is the colouring of a monarch butterfly?

4 What is a fer-de-lance?

5 King of Saxony and Princess Stephania's are varieties of what?

6 What is the alternative common name for the fish hawk?

7 What are ungulates?

8 What is anabolism?

9 Through which two arteries does blood leave the human heart?

10 Which unusual feature is shared by the frigatebird and the siamang?

11 What is a deodar?

12 Identify these cloud forms from their standard abbreviations: Ci, St, Cb?

13 Which element is a constituent of all proteins but not of carbohydrates?

14 How does carbon monoxide affect the body?

15 Which living fish was discovered in 1938 - 60 million years after its supposed extinction?

1 What is the largest freshwater mammal?

2 What are the two species of camel?

3 What is a leucocyte?

4 What is a kissing gourami?

5 Which creature has the Latin name *Indicator indicator*?

6 To which bird family does the snipe belong?

7 What is a dabbling duck?

8 Of which animal are there three species - Burchell's, Grevy's and mountain?

9 What is *Drosophila melanogaster* and why is it important?

10 What are cocci and bacilli?

11 What are chiroptera?

12 What are mudskippers noted for?

13 What is myelin?

14 Why do birds swallow grit?

15 What is a nephron?

1 Where does the European freshwater eel spawn?

2 What are the four bones of the leg?

3 What name is given to the fin at the end of a fish's tail?

4 What causes gout?

5 Where would you find a sugar glider?

6 What are the longest cells in the human body?

7 What is Jacobson's organ?

8 What is an onager?

9 What is the modern science of ethology concerned with?

10 What is a detrivore?

11 What is a Tasmanian devil?

12 In what way does the guppy fish resemble a mammal?

13 How many bones are there in the human hand?

14 What are the three kinds of setter?

15 What is the *corpus callosum*?

1 What is the largest lizard?

2 Where is ambergris (a traditional ingredient of fine perfume) formed?

3 What is the lithosphere?

4 Where, in the human body, is the pineal gland?

5 In which phylum are starfish placed?

6 What is the biggest fish?

7 Which part of the brain connects with the spinal cord?

8 Which deer is sometimes known as the barking deer?

9 What is *Helix pomatia*?

10 What is nagana?

11 What is the colouring of the adult Colorado potato beetle?

12 What is the common name for the unusual looking monkey *Nasalis larvatus*?

13 Where are the world's lemurs found?

14 How many cranial nerves are there in the human body?

15 What are the Van Allen belts?

1 What does the basking shark feed on?

2 What is the Earth's core thought mainly to consist of?

3 What is the medical significance of lamb, cauliflower and pears?

4 What is spirogyra?

5 Which acid builds up in the human body during exercise?

6 What is the longest living snake?

7 What are smews?

8 What is the function of the lateral line in the body of a fish?

9 What is a piddock?

10 What is dangerous about a teratogenic substance?

11 What is the meaning of the name of the protein deficiency disease kwashiorkor?

12 What is plasmalemma?

13 What is unusual about the reproductive behaviour of a seahorse?

14 What do saprophytes feed on?

15 What are Einkorn, Emmer and Shot?

1 From which goat is mohair obtained? ✓

2 What kind of flowers are cattleyas?

3 What is *Rana temporaria*?

4 Which basic feature distinguishes true flies from most other insects?

5 What is the lowest region of the Earth's atmosphere?

6 In which part of the human body is the thymus?

7 What is the largest poisonous snake in Africa? ✓

8 By what term is bilharzia also known, and what causes the disease?

9 What is the colouring of the ratel (honey badger)?

10 What is remarkable about the evolution of the ginkgo tree?

11 What is Minamata disease?

12 How does an ant lion catch its prey?

13 What is a geophyte?

14 What is a fennec?

15 What is notable about a swiftlet's nest?

1 In which part of the tongue are the sour receptors concentrated?

2 For what animal is Przewalski famous?

3 To which phylum does man belong?

4 What is a microphagous animal?

5 Which bird is known as the laughing jackass? ✓

6 What is a tigon?

7 What is successively a parr, a smolt and a grilse?

8 Where is the musk ox found?

9 Which species of dolphin is the popular performer in marine parks?

10 Where would you find an atlas on an axis?

11 In what fundamental way does a shark differ from a cod?

12 Typical insects have two sets of jaws. What are they called?

13 What is Britain's rarest amphibian?

14 Which three elements are constituents of most fertilisers as they are of primary importance to plant growth?

15 Where are armadillos found?

1 *Papio sphinx* is a strikingly coloured baboon. What is its common name?

2 Which British tree lives longest?

3 What is graphite composed of?

4 What is the term for the community of organisms inhabiting the seafloor?

5 What is the snail's rasping organ called?

6 What is a baobab?

7 How does the paradoxical frog get its name?

8 What is the jejunum?

9 What is the difference between the ileum and the ilium?

10 What have bluefin, albacore and big-eyed in common?

11 What is the difference between monoecious and dioecious plants?

12 What are the two minerals designated by the word jade?

13 What is the function of rods in the eye?

14 What is the basic difference between a virus and a bacterium?

15 Where is myxomatosis indigenous?

1 What name is given to the domesticated albino polecat?

2 What is the alternative name for the rockfowl?

3 What would you lose during a cholecystectomy?

4 To which order do ducks, geese and swans belong?

5 Lack of which chemical compound is associated with Parkinson's disease?

6 What is a markhor?

7 The following are among the ten minerals used as an index of hardness on Mohs' scale. Arrange in order of increasing hardness: topaz, gypsum, apatite and quartz?

8 What is the closest relative to the duck-billed platypus?

9 What are the three ways in which bees are known to communicate?

10 Which mammal has the longest gestation period?

11 What are the two parts of a lichen?

12 What is the highly distinctive marking on the abdomen of the black widow spider (*Lactrodectus mactans*)?

13 Why is the sensitive plant so called?

14 To which order does the mayfly belong?

15 Which metal forms part of the chlorophyll molecule?

NATURE QUESTIONS

1 Where do pugs originate?

2 What is the commonly used term for a tsunami?

3 Of which vulture are there two species - the Andean and the Californian?

4 Which dietary deficiency causes pellagra?

5 What is the Latin name for the brown rat?

6 What are edentates?

7 What name is given to parallel banded agate in shades of white with black, brown or red?

8 What are ratites?

9 From which rodent is the fur musquash obtained?

10 Where is the hyoid bone?

11 What is the largest living wild sheep?

12 Place these prehistoric periods in chronological order: Ordovician, Devonian, Silurian, Cambrian.

13 Where in nature would you find stridulation?

14 Place in order: family, phylum, species, kingdom, class, order, genus.

15 Which primate is sometimes known as a tree bear, bush bear or softly-softly?

NATURE ANSWERS

1 The cuttlefish.
2 A third eyelid.
3 They are dogs which cannot bark.
4 Pikas.
5 They destroy cereals such as oats, rye, barley and wheat.
6 They were used to hunt woodcocks.
7 Seven.
8 A bulldog and a terrier.
9 Crocodiles, alligators and caymens, and gavials.
10 *Solanum tuberosum.*
11 The hog-nosed (or bumblebee) bat.
12 Small wingless insects found throughout the world.
13 Elephants - they are associated with the condition 'musth' or elephant rage.
14 The main ore of tin.
15 The coriolis force.

1 The ostrich and the bee hummingbird of Cuba.
2 *Pasteurella pestis* (*Yersinia pestis*).
3 A common seaweed.
4 Saffron.
5 The wolverine.
6 A gelatinous substance in the eyeball.
7 Calcium and potassium.
8 Blood vessels and nerves through bone.
9 Varieties of potato.
10 *Gallus gallus* - the red jungle fowl.
11 Lack of iodine.
12 Its huge nest - sometimes six feet across and four feet high.
13 One which is very well developed on hatching and therefore capable of leaving the nest almost immediately.
14 The arm.
15 From the resemblance of its crest to a bunch of quills behind a clerk's ear.

1 A type of fungus which grows on leaves after they have been chewed and stored by the ants.
2 Yellow.
3 Rosaceae.
4 It means 'badger dog' - they were originally bred to chase badgers underground.
5 The okapi.
6 Under normal circumstances it retains larval characteristics throughout its life.
7 The cerebellum.
8 Acacia.
9 The process by which a living cell duplicates itself exactly by dividing.
10 It captures above-the-surface insects by expelling a jet of water.
11 Beetles (250,000 to 300,000 known species).
12 Garnet.
13 The selective growth of a plant towards the pull of gravity.
14 Lachrymal glands.
15 A volcanic vent that issues vapours and gases.

4

1 The liver.
2 A wild llama.
3 Orange and black, with white spots.
4 A particularly venomous snake of the viper family.
5 Birds of paradise.
6 Osprey.
7 Hoofed mammals.
8 The building-up of living matter from nutrients.
9 The aorta and the pulmonary artery.
10 An inflatable throat sac.
11 A Himalayan cedar highly prized for its fragrant, durable timber.
12 Cirrus, stratus, and cumulonimbus.
13 Nitrogen.
14 It combines irreversibly with haemoglobin thus impairing the blood's ability to transport oxygen from the lungs.
15 The coelacanth.

NATURE **ANSWERS**

5

1 The hippopotamus.
2 Bactrian and dromedary (Arabian).
3 A white blood cell.
4 A fish.
5 The greater honey-guide - a bird that indicates the location of bees' nests.
6 *Scolopacidae* (sandpipers).
7 One which feeds around the surface of the water.
8 The zebra.
9 The fruit fly. It has been used extensively in genetics experiments.
10 Cocci are rounded bacteria. Bacilli are rod-like bacteria.
11 Bats.
12 Theyare fish that can manoeuvre successfully out of water.
13 The fatty insulating coating of nerves.
14 To enable them to grind food in their gizzard.
15 A filtering unit in the kidney. A normal human kidney contains over a million.

6

1 The Sargasso sea.
2 The femur, patella, fibula and tibia.
3 Caudal fin.
4 Excess of uric acid in the blood.
5 In Australia. It is a small tree-dwelling marsupial.
6 Neurones (nerve cells).
7 An organ of smell in the mouths of snakes and some other animals.
8 An Asian wild ass.
9 The study of animal behaviour.
10 An animal that feeds on dead matter such as leaves or animal remains.
11 A ferocious marsupial found in Tasmania.
12 It bears live young.
13 27.
14 The English, the Gordon, and the Irish or Red.
15 The bridge of nerve tissue linking the left and right hemispheres of the brain.

1 The giant monitor lizard, commonly known as the Komodo dragon.
2 In the intestines of the sperm whale.
3 The outer regions of the Earth's crust.
4 Inside the forehead.
5 Echinodermata.
6 The whale shark - which can reach 60ft in length and 40 tons in weight.
7 The medulla oblongata.
8 The muntjac.
9 The Roman or edible snail (*escargot*).
10 A disease of cattle and horses spread by the tsetse fly.
11 Yellowish-orange to red with black stripes on its wing-cases.
12 The proboscis monkey.
13 Madagascar and nearby islands.
14 Twelve pairs.
15 Two doughnut-shaped zones of electrically charged particles which encircle the earth.

1 Plankton.
2 Iron.
3 They are foods to which people are rarely allergic, so they are used in elimination diets to determine the cause of an allergy.
4 A filamentous green algae.
5 Lactic acid.
6 The reticulated python.
7 Small diving ducks.
8 It is a fluid filled canal along the flanks which detects water-borne vibration.
9 A marine bivalve capable of boring into rock and shells.
10 It can cause birth deformities.
11 'Displaced child' - ie, a child deprived of its mother's milk by a new baby and therefore starved.
12 The membranous wall which surrounds living cells.
13 The male carries and hatches the eggs.
14 Dead organic matter. They are plants which are incapable of photosynthesis.
15 Varieties of wheat.

1 Angora.
2 Orchids.
3 The common European frog.
4 True flies have only one pair of full wings; most other insects have two.
5 The troposphere.
6 The base of the neck. It is involved in the immune system during childhood.
7 The black mamba (*Dendroaspis*).
8 Schistosomiasis. The various forms of the disease are caused by parasitic flatworms, often called flukes.
9 The upper body is grey and the underside is black.
10 It is a 'living fossil' - sole survivor of a group dating back approximately 250 million years.
11 Mass mercury poisoning due to pollution. It is named after Minamata, Japan, the site of a serious outbreak.
12 It constructs a steep-sided conical pit and waits at the bottom.
13 A plant which survives winter by re-growing from an underground structure such as a bulb.
14 A small long-eared fox.
15 It is made from saliva and used in bird's nest soup.

1 The edges.
2 Przewalski's horse - the last surviving subspecies of wild horse.
3 Chordata.
4 One which feeds on minute particles such as algae.
5 The kookaburra.
6 A hybrid between a tiger and a lion.
7 A young salmon.
8 In arctic regions of North America and North Greenland.
9 The bottlenose dolphin.
10 In the human neck. They are the first two vertebrae supporting the skull.
11 The former has a skeleton of cartilage; that of the latter is bony.
12 Mandibles and maxillae.
13 The natterjack toad.
14 Nitrogen, phosphorus and potassium.
15 In the Americas from Argentina to the Southern USA.

1 The mandrill.
2 The common yew (*Taxus baccata*).
3 Carbon.
4 Benthos.
5 The radula.
6 An African tree remarkable for the thickness of its trunk.
7 The adult frog is shorter than the tadpole.
8 Part of the gut below the stomach.
9 The ileum is part of the digestive system but the ilium is a bone.
10 They are all tuna.
11 The former have the male and female reproductive organs on separate flowers on the same plant; the latter have them on different plants.
12 Nephrite and jadeite.
13 They are responsible for vision in dim light.
14 Unlike a bacterium a virus has no metabolism and so can only reproduce in a host cell.
15 South America. It was deliberately introduced to Australia and western Europe to control the rabbit population.

12

1 Ferret.
2 Bald crow.
3 Your gall bladder.
4 Anseriformes.
5 Dopamine.
6 A wild goat.
7 Gypsum (2), apatite (5), quartz (7), topaz (8).
8 The spiny anteater.
9 Touch, smell (scent secretions) and mime (dance).
10 The Asiatic elephant.
11 An alga and a fungus in a symbiotic relationship.
12 A red marking often in the shape of an hour-glass.
13 It folds its leaves when touched.
14 Ephemeroptera.
15 Magnesium.

NATURE ANSWERS

1 China.

2 Tidal wave.

3 The condor.

4 Lack of niacin.

5 *Rattus norvegicus.*

6 An order of mammals (including sloths, armadillos and true anteaters) whose teeth are unusual or absent.

7 Onyx.

8 Flightless running birds such as the ostrich that lack a keeled breast-bone.

9 The muskrat.

10 In the throat.

11 The argali of central Asia.

12 Cambrian, Ordovician, Silurian, Devonian.

13 Among animals such as crickets which produce sounds by rubbing parts of their bodies together.

14 Species, genus, family, order, class, phylum, kingdom.

15 The potto (*Perodicticus potto*).

COMPETITION QUESTIONS

1 What are the five classics of English horseracing?

2 Which five boxers beat Muhammed Ali in professional fights? ✓

3 Which British showjumper won the individual three-day event at the 1972 Olympics?

4 Who was Britain's first £100,000 Rugby League player?

5 Whom did Rocky Marciano defeat to become heavyweight champion of the world?

6 To the nearest five seconds, what was the speed skating world record for 500 metres at the beginning of 1986?

7 Which sport is supposed to have been influenced by the sight of a monkey's agility?

8 Which men won Olympic marathons in 1976, 1980 and 1984?

9 In which sport has the greatest number of official world records been broken by a single man?

10 Which golfer won the British Open, US Open and the US Masters in 1953?

11 Which horse ran the fastest Epsom Derby?

12 Name the eleven members of the England football team that won the World Cup final?

13 For which teams did Sir Alf Ramsey play football?

14 What was the name of the runner nicknamed 'the flying Finn'?

15 Who were the last four British women to win the Wimbledon singles final?

COMPETITION QUESTIONS

1 Who was the first British player to win the European Golden Boot?

2 What are the two lifts used in Olympic weightlifting?

3 Who was the first player to score one hundred points in a game in an American National Basketball Association match?

4 Which race is known as the 'French Derby'?

5 What is the record for consecutive wins in English League football?

6 Which dog won the 1986 Greyhound Derby?

7 What was *paganica*?

8 Which footballer played in five successive soccer World Cup tournaments?

9 What unique Olympic record does Alfred Oerter hold?

10 How many players are there in a lacrosse team?

11 Which bullfighter received the title "The man who derailed the bull"?

12 What are the Old, the New, the Eden and the Jubilee?

13 What is the highest belt that has been awarded in judo?

14 In the American National Football League which cities are represented by the Browns, the Lions and the Seahawks?

15 Who managed the English football team for the longest period?

1 Who won the first Super Bowl and when?

2 In Rugby League, what points are awarded for a try, a goal and a drop goal?

3 What unique Olympic treble did Emil Zatopek achieve?

4 What was the subject of Roger Ascham's 1545 treatise *Toxophilus*?

5 Name the 1985, 1986 and 1987 Derby winners.

6 Who set a world record of 6.0 metres for the pole vault?

7 In which sport would you compete for the MacRobertson International Shield?

8 What are the Queen's racing colours?

9 Who compete for the Bermuda Bowl?

10 What was Britain's most successful Olympic bobsleigh duo?

11 How did the swimmer Capt. Matthew Webb die?

12 In archery, what do the initials of the French world governing body FITA stand for?

13 Apart from Liverpool, which team won the English League Championship more than once during the 1970s?

14 Who won the London to Brighton Walk eight times in succession from 1955 - 1962?

15 Who was the first man to run the 110 metres hurdles in less than 13 seconds?

1 Which footballer was the First Division's leading scorer in 1985-6?

2 What is a 'perfect deal' in bridge?

3 Which sports make up the Olympic modern pentathlon?

4 Who compete for the Curtis Cup?

5 What name is given to the traditional parade and horse race held every July and August in the centre of the city of Siena?

6 Which sports are combined in an Olympic biathlon?

7 Which footballer holds the record for scoring most goals in the final stage of the World Cup?

8 In which sport would you find a 'knuckleball'?

9 Who won the 1986 and 1987 London Marathons?

10 Which football club plays at Leeds Road?

11 At what event did Christopher Brasher win an Olympic gold medal?

12 Which players did Borg defeat to win his Wimbledon titles?

13 Who captained England in the 1970-71 Test series in which England regained the Ashes in Australia?

14 In 1972-3, who captained England to rugby victories over South Africa, New Zealand and Australia, - the first two teams being beaten on their home soil?

15 Who were Britain's last ice-dance world champions before Torvill and Dean?

1 Which jockey has won the most races?

2 Who was the first negro to become World Boxing Heavyweight champion and whom did he defeat in doing so?

3 How long did Joe Louis hold the world heavyweight championship?

4 Who holds the career record for most goals scored in the Football League?

5 Who was the first man to retain an Olympic marathon title?

6 Who defeated whom in the longest Wimbledon match?

7 How many tied test matches have there been?

8 What was patented under the name 'Sphairistiké'?

9 Where did squash originate?

10 In which Scottish game is the ball struck with a 'caman' and the goal called a 'hail'?

11 Who was dubbed the 'Peer of Wigan'?

12 Which countries have won the soccer World Cup and how many times?

13 Name the five events at which Britain won gold medals at the Summer Olympics in 1984?

14 Who holds the record for the greatest number of dismissals by a wicketkeeper in a Test match?

15 Who won three successive gold medals in the Olympic triple jump?

1 Who scored the most runs ever in a first-class cricket innings and how many?

2 What does the Fédération Internationale d'Escrime govern?

3 Whom did Alan Minter defeat to become world champion?

4 Who ran the first automatically timed sub 10-sec 100 metres that was not 'wind assisted'?

5 Where is the Cresta Run?

6 Who is traditionally believed to have invented rugby?

7 What is the longest Olympic swimming event?

8 In golf what is an 'albatross'?

9 Which team won the Super Bowl in 1985?

10 Where is the British Equestrian Centre?

11 What are 'cesta-punta' and 'remonte'?

12 Who held the World Light Heavyweight Boxing title for the longest period?

13 In 1977 who set a world record of 2.0 metres for the women's high jump?

14 Which track athlete won individual gold medals at both the 1976 and 1984 Olympics?

15 Where and when was the first sub 4-minute mile run?

1 How long is a standard squash court?

2 Who is the only man to score 2,000 runs and take 200 wickets in a season, in first class cricket?

3 What unique Olympic feat did Lasse Viren achieve?

4 Who was the first woman to run a sub 2hr 30m marathon?

5 Who first ran the 1500m in less than 3m 30seconds?

6 What was 'Chaturanga'?

7 Which races comprise the American horseracing Triple Crown?

8 Where would you find a 'Hecht dismount?'

9 How many players are there on court in basketball, volleyball and netball?

10 In a standard game of Bezique, what is a 'Bezique'?

11 Where is the Inferno raced and what is it?

12 Whom did Barry McGuigan defeat to become world champion, and to whom did he lose his title?

13 How many squares are there on a chess board?

14 Who won the British modern pentathlon championship ten times between 1963 and 1974?

15 What is Pelé's real name?

1 Which British racing driver won 25 Grand Prix races between 1962 and 1968?

2 What was Babe Ruth's full name?

3 What is a maiden race?

4 Which golfer won the 1984 U.S. Open?

5 Which teams did Nottingham Forest defeat in their two European Cup finals?

6 Over what distance is drag racing normally contested?

7 Whom did Steve Davis defeat in the finals of his four snooker world championship wins?

8 In which sport are the Swaythling and Marcel Corbillon cups competed for?

9 After whom is the ice skating jump known as an 'axel' named?

10 On which course are the first and last horse races of the flat season run?

11 Which man played in four Wimbledon singles finals and lost them all?

12 In standard five card poker, what are the statistical chances of being dealt a flush straight from the pack?

13 Who won the squash World Open Championship in 1985?

14 Who was the oldest man to play Test cricket?

15 Excluding substitutes, how many players comprise an ice hockey team?

Who said: "The ideal soccer board of directors should be made up of three men - two dead and the other dying"?

Which was the first non-American yacht to win the America's Cup?

Who said: "He's going for the pink - and for those of you with black and white sets, the yellow is behind the blue"?

Who is the only man to have been elected European Footballer of the Year three times in succession?

In rugby, which country is known as the Pumas?

Which country has won most Olympic titles in water polo?

In which position did Tony Neary play rugby for England?

What is the highest break theoretically possible in snooker?

Who was world chess champion for the longest period this century?

0 Where have the summer Olympics been held since World War II?

1 What was 'paille-maille'?

2 What is the standard weight of the shot used in shot-putting?

3 Which three men have won the Tour de France five times?

4 What is a matador's sword called?

5 In athletics, at which ages do men and women respectively qualify for official competitions as veterans?

1 How many players are there in an American and a Canadian football team?

2 Who won the world table-tennis championship, and the U.S. lawn tennis singles title three years later?

3 Who sired Sadler's Wells, Secreto and the Minstrel?

4 Which countries have reached the football World Cup final?

5 Who is the 'Great White Shark'?

6 At which ground do Burnley play football and what is the club nickname?

7 Who won the first Embassy world professional darts championship in 1978?

8 In which sport did Alexander J.Cartwright devise the basic modern rules, in 1845?

9 For which teams did Jimmy Greaves play?

10 Who won a world championship on Beethoven?

11 In which sport was Chuang Tse-tung an outstanding player?

12 Who won a record number of 15 motor cycling world championship titles between 1968 and 1975?

13 What does 'karate' mean?

14 Which two men have each won two Olympic decathlons?

15 Who share the record for the fastest century scored in first-class cricket?

What is the name of the stadium of the Los Angeles Rams?

Where were the first Winter Olympics held?

In horseracing, what is the maximum age of a filly?

Which countries have won the most Olympic team titles in men nd women's gymnastics?

Who skippered 'Stars and Stripes' in its 1987 America's Cup ictory?

Who scored for Manchester United when they became the first nglish team to win the European Cup?

Who was the first boxer to regain the world heavyweight hampionship?

Which footballer won FA Cup winners' medals in 1978 and 1979, laying for different teams?

In which sport are the Uber and Thomas cups contested?

) In which sport has Britain's Malcolm Cooper set world records?

l Which Britons have won the World Grand Prix motor racing hampionship?

2 Since World War II who is the only man to have won the Olympic 00m and 1500m in the same year?

3 What is the exact length of the marathon?

4 How many classics did Lester Piggott win as a jockey?

5 Name the events of the Olympic decathlon.

1 Which athletics world record, set in 1935, was unbroken until 1960?

2 How does a cricket umpire signal a bye?

3 For what achievement is a Lonsdale belt awarded outright?

4 Who was the only person to defend successfully a 100 metres Olympic title?

5 What is the Doggett's Coat and Badge?

6 Which athletes gave controversial black power salutes at the 1968 Olympics?

7 Which speed skater won five Olympic gold medals in 1980?

8 From which three stallions can English Thoroughbreds trace their ancestry in the male line?

9 Who was the last Briton to play in a Wimbledon men's singles semi-final?

10 Which players have won the lawn tennis grand slam?

11 Who won the men's sprint double at the 1972 Olympics?

12 Which sporting association do the initials BCGBA refer to?

13 Of which game are 'Ring Taw', 'Spangy' and 'Capture' forms?

14 How many players are there in a Gaelic Football side?

15 What are 'trench', 'skeet' and 'down the line'?

1 What is the French name for real (or royal) tennis?

2 Which sport is associated with the St Louis Blues?

3 Which sport is played with brooms and stones?

4 Who played football for England and Arsenal and cricket for England and Middlesex?

5 Which cricketer scored the most runs in first-class cricket?

6 What is the world record for the long jump?

7 Which teams won the first three F A Cup finals?

8 In harness racing, what is the difference between a trotter and a pacer?

9 What is spelunking?

10 To the nearest five runs, what was Sir Donald Bradman's Test-match average?

11 Who won the 1985 world professional billiards championship?

12 Which athlete was recognised as an Olympic champion in 1982 - 29 years after his death?

13 Which footballer played 150 times for Peru?

14 Which team consists of a Lead, Second, Third and Skip?

15 Which sport is associated with the name Jill Hammersley?

COMPETITION ANSWERS

1 Oaks, St Leger, Derby, 1000 Guineas and 2000 Guineas.

2 Joe Frazier, Ken Norton, Leon Spinks, Larry Holmes, Trevor Berbick.

3 Richard Meade

4 Joe Lydon who moved from Widnes to Wigan in 1986.

5 Jersey Joe Walcott.

6 36.49 seconds, by Igor Zhelezovsky.

7 Kung fu.

8 W.Cierpinski of E.Germany in 1976 and 1980 and C.Lopes of Portugal in 1984.

9 Weightlifting. Between 1970 and 1977 Vasili Alexeyev of the Soviet Union broke eighty world records.

10 Ben Hogan.

11 Mahmoud in 1936.

12 Banks, Cohen, Wilson, Stiles, J.Charlton, Moore, Ball, Hurst, R.Charlton, Hunt, Peters.

13 Southampton, Tottenham and England.

14 Paavo Nurmi.

15 Dorothy Round (1937), Angela Mortimer (1961), Ann Jones (1969), Virginia Wade (1977).

1 Ian Rush in 1983-4.

2 The 'snatch' and the 'clean and jerk'.

3 Wilt 'the Stilt' Chamberlain.

4 The Prix du Jockey Club run at Chantilly in June over the Derby distance of 1½ miles.

5 14 - by Bristol City, Manchester United and Preston North End.

6 Tico.

7 A Roman game played with a feather-stuffed ball.

8 The goalkeeper Antonio Carbajal of Mexico between 1950 and 1966.

9 He won discus gold medals in four consecutive Olympics, between 1956 and 1968.

10 10 for men, 12 for women.

11 Juan Belmonte.

12 Golf courses at St Andrews.

13 The red belt (10th dan) - only thirteen men have won it.

14 Cleveland, Detroit and Seattle.

15 Walter Winterbottom - from 1946-62.

COMPETITION **ANSWERS**

1 The Green Bay Packers in 1967.
2 3-2-1.
3 Gold medals in the 5,000 metres, 10,000 metres and marathon in the same games - in 1952.
4 Archery.
5 Slip Anchor, Shahrastani, Reference Point.
6 Sergei Bubka of the Soviet Union in 1985.
7 Croquet.
8 Purple bodice with gold braid, scarlet sleeves, and a black cap with gold fringe.
9 Bridge players, for the world championship.
10 Robin Dixon and Anthony Nash who won a gold medal in 1964.
11 He drowned while attempting to swim the rapids of Niagara Falls.
12 Fédération Internationale de Tir à l'Arc.
13 Derby County in 1971-2 and 1974-5.
14 Don Thompson.
15 Renaldo Nehemiah.

1 Gary Lineker
2 Each of the four players receives a complete suit.
Odds against are 2, 235, 197, 406, 895, 366, 368, 301, 559, 991, to 1.
3 Cross country running, shooting, swimming, fencing and show-jumping.
4 Women golfers of Great Britain and Ireland against the USA.
5 The Palio.
6 Skiing and shooting.
7 Just Fontaine with 13 goals in 1958 for France. (Gerd Müller scored an aggregate of 14 goals in 1970 and 74).
8 It's a type of pitch in baseball.
9 Toshihiko Seko and Grete Waitz in 1986. Hiroma Taniguchi and Ingrid Christiansen in 1987.
10 Huddersfield Town.
11 3,000 metres steeplechase.
12 I.Nastase, J. Connors, (twice), L. R. Tanner, J. P. McEnroe.
13 Ray Illingworth.
14 John Pullin.
15 Bernard Ford and Diane Towler from 1966-9.

1 Willie Shoemaker.
2 Jack Johnson in 1908 by beating Tommy Burns.
3 11 years 8 months.
4 Arthur Rowley of W.B.A., Fulham, Leicester and Shrewsbury. 434 goals between 1946 and 1965.
5 Abebe Bikila of Ethiopia at Tokyo in 1964.
6 Ricardo Gonzales defeated Charlie Pasarell in 1969 in a match of 112 games.
7 Two. India v Australia in 1986 and Australia v W. Indies in 1960.
8 Lawn Tennis, in 1874 by Major W. C. Wingfield.
9 At Harrow School in the 19th century.
10 Shinty.
11 The rugby player Billy Boston of Wigan and Great Britain.
12 Uruguay (twice), Italy (three times), Brazil (three times), England (once), W.Germany (twice), Argentina(twice).
13 Decathlon, men's 1500 metres, women's javelin, rowing (fours with coxswain), shooting (small bore rifle).
14 R.W. Taylor with ten wickets for England, against India in 1980.
15 Victor Saneyev of the USSR in 1968, 1972 and 1976.

6

1 Hanif Mohammad scored 499 for Karachi v Bahawalpur in 1959.
2 Fencing.
3 Vito Antuofermo.
4 Jim Hines.
5 St Moritz, Switzerland.
6 William Webb Ellis.
7 1500 metres.
8 Three strokes under par.
9 The San Francisco 49ers.
10 Stoneleigh, Warwickshire.
11 Forms of pelota.
12 Archie Moore, from 1952-61.
13 Rosemarie Ackermann of E.Germany.
14 Edwin Moses at the 400 metres hurdles.
15 The Iffley Road track, Oxford in May 1954.

1 32 feet.
2 G.H. Hirst of Yorkshire in 1906.
3 He won the 5,000 and 10,000 metres 'double' at successive Olympics.
4 Grete Waitz in 1978.
5 Steve Cram, in 1985 at Nice.
6 An Indian game from which chess is said to be derived.
7 Kentucky Derby, Belmont Stakes, Preakness Stakes.
8 In gymnastics.
9 10, 12 and 14.
10 A scoring combination of a Jack of Diamonds and a Queen of Spades.
11 In Switzerland. It is the longest downhill skiing race - of over 8 miles - starting at the top of the Schilthorn.
12 Eusebio Pedroza and Steve Cruz.
13 64.
14 Jim Fox.
15 Edson Arantes do Nascimento.

1 Jim Clark.
2 George Herman Ruth.
3 A race for horses that have never won.
4 Fuzzy Zoeller.
5 Malmo and Hamburg.
6 ¼ of a mile.
7 D.Mountjoy (1981), C.Thorburn (1983), J.White (1984), and J.Johnson(1987).
8 Table tennis.
9 The Norwegian skater Axel Paulsen.
10 Doncaster.
11 Ken Rosewall.
12 0.1956%.
13 Jahangir Khan of Pakistan.
14 Wilfred Rhodes - for England against the West Indies in 1930 - at the age of 52.
15 Six.

COMPETITION ANSWERS

1 Tommy Docherty.

2 Australia II in 1983.

3 Ted Lowe, the TV snooker commentator.

4 Michel Platini.

5 Argentina.

6 Hungary - six wins.

7 Flanker.

8 155. It begins with a 'free ball' in which a colour is potted as a 'red', then the black is potted and then the table is cleared.

9 Emanuel Lasker, from 1900 - 1921. His reign began in 1894.

10 London, Helsinki, Melbourne, Rome, Tokyo, Mexico City, Munich, Montreal, Moscow, Los Angeles.

11 A game played with a wooden mallet and wooden ball.

12 16 lb for men. 8 lb 13 oz for women.

13 Jacques Anquetil (of France), Eddy Merckx (of Belgium), Bernard Hinault (of France).

14 An estoque.

15 35 for women and 40 for men.

1 11 and 12.

2 Fred Perry.

3 Northern Dancer.

4 Uruguay, Italy, Brazil, England, W.Germany, Argentina, Czechoslovakia, Hungary, Sweden, Holland.

5 The golfer Greg Norman.

6 Turf Moor, and 'the Clarets'.

7 Leighton Rees of Wales.

8 Baseball.

9 A.C. Milan, Chelsea, Tottenham and West Ham.

10 David Broome - in 1970.

11 Table tennis.

12 Giacomo Agostini.

13 Empty hand.

14 R. Mathias in 1948 and 1952, and D.Thompson in 1980 and 1984.

15 Percy Fender for Surrey in 1920, and Steven O'Shaughnessy for Lancashire in 1983. Both in 35 mins.

1 Anaheim Stadium.
2 Chamonix, France in 1924.
3 Four years.
4 Japan won the men's title five times, and the USSR won the women's title eight times.
5 Denis Conner.
6 Charlton (2), Best and Kidd - in beating Benfica 4-1.
7 Floyd Patterson - who lost the title to Ingemar Johansson and then won it back from him.
8 Brian Talbot- for Ipswich and Arsenal.
9 Badminton.
10 Rifle shooting.
11 Mike Hawthorn, Graham Hill, Jim Clark, John Surtees, Jackie Stewart and James Hunt.
12 Peter Snell of New Zealand in 1964.
13 26 miles 385 yards.
14 29.
15 100 metres, long jump, shot put, high jump, 400 metres, 110 metres hurdles, discus, pole vault, javelin, 1500 metres.

12

1 Jesse Owens' record of 8.13m for the long jump.
2 By raising a open hand above the head.
3 The winning of three British title fights in the same division by a boxer.
4 Wyomia Tyus of the USA in 1968, (Archie Hahn did so- but at the intercalated games of 1906).
5 A rowing race, held annually on the Thames since 1716.
6 Tommie Smith and John Carlos.
7 Eric Heiden.
8 The Byerley Turk, the Darley Arabian and the Godolphin Arabian (or Godolphin Barb).
9 Roger Taylor - in 1973, and previously - 1970.
10 Donald Budge, Rod Laver (twice), Maureen Connolly, Margaret Court and Martina Navratilova.
11 Valeri Borzov.
12 The British Crown Green Bowling Association.
13 Marbles.
14 15.
15 Forms of clay pigeon shooting.

1 Jeu de paume.

2 Ice hockey.

3 Curling.

4 Denis Compton.

5 Sir Jack Hobbs - 61,237 at an average ·· 50.65.

6 29ft 2½in (8.9m) achieved by Bob Beamon in 1968.

7 The Wanderers - twice, and Oxford University.

8 A trotter works its diagonally opposite legs in unison whereas a pacer moves both left legs in unison and then both right legs.

9 The sport of exploring caves.

10 99.94.

11 Ray Edmonds.

12 Jim Thorpe - he was officially reinstated as a champion after being stripped of his medals (decathlon and pentathlon golds) in 1912 for professionalism.

13 Hector Chumpitaz between 1963 and 1982.

14 A team of four players in bowls.

15 Table tennis.

A

Q.A1 **Who designed this building?**
Q.A2 **In which city is it?**
Q.A3 **What is its name?**
Q.A4 **Which mountain in Catalonia – named for its jagged pinnacles – is sometimes said to have inspired its design?**

Q.B1 **What is the name of this sportsman whose aggressive bowling during the England cricket team's 1932/3 tour of Australia was the focus of a major controversy?**
Q.B2 **Which English county did he play for?**
Q.B3 **What name is given to the bowling technique he adopted during the tour?**
Q.B4 **Who was the England captain who devised this intimidating technique as a means of countering the menace of Bradman and regaining the Ashes?**
Q.B5 **By which euphemistic term was this bowling tactic referred to by its advocates?**

B

Q.C1 **Which film director, who died in 1978, is shown here and who was his father?**

Q.C2 **Which film by this director – regarded as a failure when premiered in 1939 – was cut, banned, had its negatives lost and was not shown to the general public in its full version until 1965, but is now considered a great masterpiece?**

Q.D1 **Identify country 1**
Q.D2 **Identify country 2**
Q.D3 **Identify country 3**
Q.D4 **Identify country 4**
Q.D5 **Identify country 5**
Q.D6 **Identify country 6**

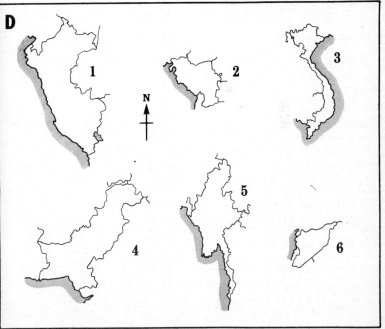

Q.E1 Who is she, and who was her eldest daughter with whom she founded the WSPU – an organisation that bore the slogan "deeds not words"?

Q.E2 What did the initials WSPU stand for?

Q.E3 Which daughter became an ardent campaigner for the independence of Ethiopia and died there in 1960?

Q.E4 For which political party was the person in the picture adopted as a prospective parliamentary candidate in 1926?

Q.E5 What was the 'Cat and Mouse' Act?

Q.F1 Who is the well-known person in this photo?

Q.G1 This person is not usually seen with a beard. Who is it?

Q.H1 Who is the actress impersonating Theda Bara?

PICTURES QUESTIONS

I

J

K

Q.I1 What is this musical instrument?

Q.J1 The instrument in the picture is a sort of bass oboe which is named after its German inventor. What is it called?

Q.K1 What is this musical instrument?

Q.L1 This is the top of a famous London landmark. Name it.

Q.M1 This is a picture of Thomas Edison's phonograph. In which decade was it invented?
Q.M2 Which material did Edison use as the first recording medium?
Q.M3 What were the first words recorded on the phonograph?

L

M

Q.N1 Who is this and what is he preparing to demonstrate?
Q.N2 In which decade was it first shown to the public?
Q.N3 What was the machine known as?

Q.O1 This animal is a very rare primate. What is it called?
Q.O2 Where is it found?
Q.O3 The middle finger of each hand is particularly long and thin. For what use is it adapted?
Q.O4 How does it locate its food?

Q.P1 Who is the woman in the picture who married her distant cousin and was given away at her wedding by her uncle who held the same high office as her husband was to achieve?

Q.P2 In what official capacity was she instrumental in the drafting and adoption of which famous UN declaration?

Q.R1 Who are the two stars and in which film are they seen here?

Q.R2 Who wrote the songs to the film?

Q.R3 Which duet do they perform in the film whilst dressed as tramps?

Q.S1 **Who are they?**
Q.S2 **Which of them won a record number of world champion driving titles and how many?**
Q.S3 **What is the nationality of the person referred to in the previous question?**

Q.T1 **What is this astronomical phenomenon?**

PICTURES ANSWERS

A1 Antonio Gaudí.
A2 Barcelona
A3 Casa Milá.
A4 Montserrat.

B1 Harold Larwood.
B2 Nottinghamshire.
B3 Bodyline.
B4 Douglas Jardine.
B5 Leg theory.

Q.C1 Jean Renoir, his father was Pierre Auguste Renoir.
Q.C2 *La Règle du Jeu.*

D1 Peru
D2 Yugoslavia
D3 Vietnam
D4 Pakistan
D5 Burma
D6 Syria

E1 Mrs Emmeline Pankhurst and Dame Christabel Harriette Pankhurst.
E2 Women's Social and Political Union.
E3 Sylvia Pankhurst.
E4 The Conservative Party.
E5 The popular name given to the Prisoners Temporary Discharge for Ill-Health Act of 1913, by which hunger-striking suffragettes could be released and then re-imprisoned without further trial if the offence was committed again.

F1 Margaret Thatcher – Front row 4th from right.

G1 Prince Philip.

H1 Marilyn Monroe.

I1 A hurdy-gurdy.

J1 A heckelphone.

K1 A serpent.

L1 The House of Commons clock tower (Big Ben).

M1 The 1870s.
M2 Tinfoil – wrapped around a cylinder.
M3 "Mary had a little lamb."

N1 John Logie Baird, television.
N2 The 1920s.
N3 A televisor.

O1 An aye-aye.
O2 In the rain forests of Madagascar.
O3 To extract insect larvae from wood.
O4 By listening. If it cannot hear the larvae chewing within the wood it taps with its fingers and listens for hollows.

P1 Eleanor Roosevelt.
P2 She was chairman of the UN Commission on Human Rights when it drafted the Universal Declaration of Human Rights of 1948.

R1 Fred Astaire and Judy Garland in *Easter Parade.*
R2 Irving Berlin.
R3 'A Couple of Swells'.

S1 Jackie Stewart and Juan Manuel Fangio.
S2 Juan Manuel Fangio – five titles during the 1950s.
S3 Argentinian.

T1 The Horsehead Nebula.